TEACHING
DAD TO
COOK
FLAPJACK

TEACHING DAD TO COOK FLAPJACK

simple recipes from a family life

MIRANDA GARDINER

hardie grant books

MELBOURNE · LONDON

In memory of my mother,
Rosalind (1949–2005), who
taught *me* to cook flapjack

Teaching Dad to Cook Flapjack
by Miranda Gardiner

First published in 2010 by Hardie
Grant Books (London) Limited
www.hardiegrant.co.uk

British Library Cataloguing-in-
Publication Data. A catalogue record
for this book is available from the
British Library.

ISBN 978-1-74066-877-4

Editor Salima Hirani
Designer Miranda Harvey
Publisher Jane Aspden
Colour reproduction by
Splitting Image Colour Studio

Printed and bound in China by
C&C Offset Printing

10 9 8 7 6 5 4 3 2 1

contents

List of recipes

Soups

Salads

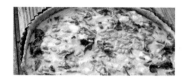

Brunches and light lunches

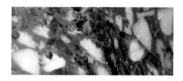

Things for tea

Weights

30g	1oz	175g	6oz	340g	12oz
55g	2oz	200g	7oz	365g	13oz
85g	3oz	225g	8oz	400g	14oz
110g	4oz	250g	9oz	420g	15oz
125g	4½oz	280g	10oz	450g	1lb
140g	5oz	310g	11oz	1kg	2¼lb

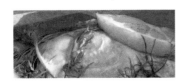

Main courses

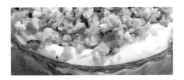

Puddings

Dressings

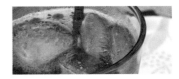

Drinks

Volumes

60ml	2fl oz (4 tbsps)	250ml	8fl oz	600ml	1 pint
75ml	2½fl oz	300ml	10fl oz (½ pint)	750ml	1¼ pints
90ml	3fl oz	360ml	12fl oz	900ml	1½ pints
100ml	3½fl oz	500ml	14fl oz	1 litre	1¾ pints
120ml	4fl oz	450ml	15fl oz (¾ pint)	1.2 litres	2 pints
150ml	5fl oz (¼ pint)	500ml	16fl oz	1.5 litres	2½ pints
200ml	7fl oz				

Notes on the book

Preheating the oven for baking

Most baking recipes start with 'Preheat the oven to…' This is fine if you have made the cake in question before and are confident about whipping it up in the time it takes your cooker's green light to go off. I find that, particularly with a new recipe, my oven gets up to temperature well before I have finished the cake, which wastes loads of energy while I read and measure quantities etc. So although I am following the culinary convention of starting my baking recipes with the 'preheat' mantra, if you know your oven heats quickly or you work at a very relaxed pace, turn the oven on between finishing the mixing and just before you start licking out the bowl!

Quantities

Most of the recipes that follow will feed 4–5 people generously. This may seem out of kilter when you consider that this book was partly born of a desire to assist my father in his solo-cooking quest, but the quantities can be easily halved or, indeed, doubled and any excess can be frozen for another day. I have tried to 'normalize' shop-bought quantities where I can: by that I mean that you shouldn't end up with an unusable drizzle of buttermilk left over in the bottom of the carton from making a batch of muffins; that can't be used for anything else, and will invariably be left in the fridge going off for a couple of weeks.

Organic and local

I buy organic food as much as possible from local farm shops, such as the Riverford Farm Shop at Staverton, and single-ingredient suppliers such as the South Devon Chilli Farm and Aune Valley Meat, and from my wonderful friends Tom and Rachael Brooking at Old Cumming Organic Farm who produce herb-and-flower salad mixes and tayberry juice. I go to the quayside fish sellers in Plymouth and stock up on fresh seafood for the freezer. Visit www.farmersmarkets.net to find farm shops, pick-your-own farms and farm home-delivery services in your own area.

Specific ingredients

Butter: I always use unsalted butter.
Eggs: These are always large, organic and free-range.
Milk: I use full-fat milk.
Salt: Unless a recipe specifically calls for fine (table) salt, I recommend sea salt for these recipes. I use Maldon sea salt, and sometimes other good-quality sea salts (see page 186 for more information).

Proving dough

'Proving' refers to the process that takes place as dough rises. The yeast (leaven) ferments (leavens) the dough, causing it to rise. Prove dough in a warm place away from draughts, covered with a clean cloth.

Making shortcrust pastry

There are a good handful of tart and pie recipes in this book that call for shortcrust pastry – most commonly, for 250g shortcrust pastry. This is made using 180g plain flour, 90g cold unsalted butter, a pinch of salt and 2–3 tablespoons ice-cold water. Combine the flour, salt and butter in a food-processor and blitz until crumbly. Add the ice-cold water a little at a time until the dough comes together to form a ball. Wrap it in clingfilm and leave in the fridge for 30 minutes (or freeze for another day) while you make the filling for the tart.

When a different amount of pastry is required, the quantities of flour and butter will be provided, and the recipe will refer to the method given here.

Blind baking

Many tarts in this book have filings that don't need as much cooking as the pastry, so the pastry must be baked blind (part-cooked, before the filling is added). Blind baking also stops the pastry from absorbing as much moisture from a wet filling as it would if it were not part-cooked. To blind bake shortcrust pastry, line your tart tin with the rolled out pastry and prick it with a fork in several places to avoid pockets of air forming. Place a circle of baking parchment (cut to fit your tin) on the pastry, then pour in baking beans (or use dried pulses). Then bake as per the recipe you are following.

Teaching Dad
to cook flapjack

simple and very satisfying food

Mum and Dad married in the late '60s in a remote Cornish church. Nowadays it has a brown road sign to entice people to come and see its holy well. The day of the wedding was a sunny day at the end of August and their wedding group photo at the reception was taken from the top floor of my grandparents farmhouse, looking down to the guests assembled on a large flat area of closely mown grass that we dubbed the tennis court. During the War this was an extra veggie patch. For their wedding, Mum and Dad received a full canteen of cutlery and a dinner set of Poole pottery, as was customary then. The wedding album was always a thing of wonder to me as a child – coming from the '60s, it incorporated a few special features inside its thick, white-padded cover. As you look at the black-and-white images settled into their photo corners behind the waxy separation paper music plays, courtesy of a discreet wind-up mechanism hidden in the spine of the book.

This book was written for my dad after my mother's death two years ago. It started as a kind of informal how-to-do manual for him – he was in his sixties and learning to cook and generally fend for himself for the first time. Like many men of his generation, he never had to worry about providing himself with a cooked meal. He may have been a man who could drive a car and tell you about the inside workings of a camera, but he couldn't cook his own supper. I started by showing him how to cook some of Mum's things. The first recipe in his book was for Chewy Flapjack, which appeals both to his sweet tooth and frequent request for 'anything to go with a cup of tea?'

I cook in a fairly low-tech way – if I cook a cake, I like to make it with a bowl and spoon, and I will often be found using my hands in preference to some smart utensil. Since I was 16, when I went to stay with a French family, I have rarely, for example, used a rolling pin; they aren't so common in French kitchens. I do have one, but it seems to get used more for rolling out play dough these days. As in France, I tend to use my hands to squash and persuade the pastry or pizza dough into place. I like the rustic finish this gives and, of course, it cuts down on the washing up.

My Chewy Flapjack recipe is definitely low-tech. As I knew Dad didn't have a pair of weighing scales (what happened to Mum's unfussy, slightly yellowed, plastic Salter ones?), I showed him the quantities in something we both have in our respective houses: Moomin cups (I would say that a Moomin cup is slightly smaller than a standard British coffee mug). The whole recipe condenses neatly into 1½ cups of sugar, 3 tablespoons of golden syrup, exactly half a can of condensed milk, 4 cups of oats and a whole packet plus an extra ⅓ of butter (300g). Feel free to use cups or follow the method given on page 12 using weighing scales.

Chewy flapjack

300g butter

4 tablespoons golden syrup

340g golden caster sugar, or use
   170g golden caster sugar and
   170g rapadura sugar (see page
   186)

200ml condensed milk

500g porridge oats

makes 16 decent slices

Flapjack is something that has always been with me – undergoing a fashionable makeover each decade in our home. In the '70s, Mum made it with porridge oats, golden syrup, sugar and butter. In the '80s, it underwent a Cranksian whole-food renaissance, with jumbo oats and black treacle providing a chewier, smokier taste. I didn't eat a lot of flapjack in the '90s, when I was in my twenties – it wasn't the kind of food that did the rounds in contemporary art circles. However, now that I have a home and children, I feel once again compelled, and am regularly asked by my Dad and my children in equal measure, to make the stuff. Since I wanted something chewy, this is my version.

The flapjack can be sliced into chunky squares and left rustically unadorned to speak for itself. But using a small triangular piece of baking paper, it can be elevated to a new and exciting level. I have got into the habit (which, I admit, has been inspired by the creative cake decorating of Gerhard Jenne of the fabulous patisserie, *Konditor and Cook* in Borough Market, London) of decorating these oaty squares with dark chocolate piping. For children, I do a whole parade of ladybirds, one-eyed monsters and so on. Adults get abstract patterns and slogans (I leave the vocabulary to you).

Flapjack is at home, naturally, at school fêtes and parties, but I also seem to bring it out frequently as an end to an informal dinner or drinks parties – a sweet hit for the road home.

Preheat the oven to 160°C/gas mark 3 and line a 33cm x 23cm roasting tin with baking parchment.

In a large, heavy-based pan melt together the butter, syrup and sugar over a low heat. When they have all mingled and melted, add the condensed milk and remove from the heat. Mix in the oats until covered by the caramel mixture.

Pour the mixture into the tin and pat down with a spatula; you don't have to be too fussy about this as, in the oven, it acts like a self-levelling floor screed and forms it own perfect level. Cook for about 15–20 minutes. When the flapjack starts to brown around the edges of the tin then it's time to take it out – it will still be

relatively pale in the middle. Cut into 16 pieces when still warm, but not straight away, as it tends to 'cook' back together again.

If you would like to decorate the flapjack, let it cool, then melt some dark chocolate in a bowl over just-poured boiling water. Make piping bags out of 20cm squares of parchment paper (cut the square in half diagonally to make two triangles, then make the long side into the nozzle by rolling it up). Pipe chocolate words, smiley faces, one-eyed monsters... until the chocolate and creative flair dry up.

After my mother's death, my father had to cope not only with his and our loss and grief, but also with acquiring a completely new skill set. He quickly grew tired of baked beans on toast and supermarket stir fries and, alongside learning about banking and domestic chores, he decided to venture into cooking for himself. At first, he would get on the phone and ask basic questions such as 'How long does it take to boil some carrots?' or 'What can I do with eggs?' He'd clearly carried around a number of culinary mysteries for years, and must have believed that the world of the cook held up a hermetic barrier to men of a certain age.

It was at the end of one of those regular phone calls that he casually asked how you go about poaching an egg. He had a sepia-toned image in his head, of a '50s-style plastic egg poacher like the one my grandma used on her Rayburn at the farm. He seemed surprised that all that was needed was a pan of boiling water, an egg and an appetite and, in the same time as it took to make a cup of tea, he could have lunch. He was always relieved to hear how straightforward cooking can be and I enjoyed being part of the demystification process. After the egg-poaching challenge came more: steaming vegetables and then steaming chicken and vegetables together in a tower of newly purchased steamers.

The collection of recipes I started to gather together for him and which, ultimately, became *Teaching Dad to Cook Flapjack*, contains a blend of family recipes reflecting our ancient Cornish and newer Finnish traditions, and recipes from generous friends who cook and share with us. There is also food that has found its way from restaurants into my home. I spent my twenties working for the flamboyant Keith Floyd, with talented young chefs such as Jean-Christophe Novelli, and then in the Sydney café scene of the '90s. I retained detailed food diaries – from which recipes and ideas have slid into my more relaxed home cooking.

I've also always been something of a culinary anthropologist, as we all are in a sense, eating our way around the world, basking in the cultures of so many different countries. As an art-history student in Florence, in complete contrast to E.M. Forster's protagonist Lucy Honeychurch in *A Room with a View*, I spent more time admiring the raw produce in the market than I did studying the paintings in the Uffizi Gallery, and brought home neat pouches of chestnut flour and other goodies to share with friends and family. Similarly, from a week in New York, my favourite memory is of a take-away sushi that I ate at the top of the Empire State Building as I watched the sun set behind the city skyline.

Sometimes, the food I cook might be a direct response to a place (for example, Cliff Cake, see page160), or even dreamt up as I try to fall asleep (Dulce de Leche Ice Cream, see page 184) but, more often than not, it is the result of something I just fancy trying one particular night – meals in progress, as it were.

Dad quickly progressed from poached eggs and flapjack but, unsurprisingly, at a time of our lives that was touched by such sadness, it was usually the warmth and familiarity of comfort foods such as shepherd's pie, stew and rice pudding that became his firm favourites. Instinctively these felt like the right starting point for recipes to teach him – they would have been like familiar friends, a warm hug from his past, whether from Mum's home cooking of the '70s and '80s or early Cornish holidays at the farm in the '60s.

One of my favourite stories that Mum used to tell us was about her childhood at the farm and how, when the hunt used to come across their land, she and her sister used to capture the fox and hide it in one of the top barns, amongst the old cars and stacked kindling, until the horses and hounds had passed by. These kinds of *Famous Five*-style episodes would invariably be followed by something cooked slowly in the oven.

The shepherd's cottage

1–2 tablespoons olive oil

1 large onion (I use red), finely sliced

2 sticks celery, chopped small

2 medium carrots, diced

2 cloves garlic, chopped

500g minced beef

500g minced lamb

200g puy lentils

1 medium glass red wine

300ml beef or chicken stock

1.4kg floury potatoes (such as Maris Piper), peeled

50g butter

enough for 5–6

I used to do 'B and B' in my home. One of my more eccentric guests made it clear early on that she only liked good old British food – 'none of that foreign rubbish'. Fine. I said that I was going to make cottage pie, then remembered it was going to be a mixture of minced beef and lamb with (she'll kill me) puy lentils. In a desperate attempt to make it sound not too 'out there' I ended up calling this hybrid Shepherd's Cottage.

Puy lentils are used to thicken the gravy which, in the absence of any flour, would be a thinish beef stock on its own. They also add an earthy note to the flavour that I love and my children, who wouldn't willingly eat a plate of lentils, seem to enjoy the meat-sodden pulses.

Heat the oil in a large, heavy-based pan and add the onion, celery, carrots and garlic. Add the meats and cook until they are lightly cooked through, which will take about 15 minutes. Stir through the lentils, and then add the wine and stock. Simmer, uncovered, for about 35 minutes. Keep checking it and add more liquid if necessary.

Meanwhile, put the potatoes on to boil and, when cooked, mash with a generous slab of butter.

Preheat the oven to 200°C/gas mark 6. Assemble in the traditional way as for shepherd's pie, by placing the meat mixture at the bottom of a large ovenproof bowl and swirling and spreading the mash on top. Cook in a hot oven for 10–15 minutes. Shepherd's Cottage is delicious served on an autumn evening with some steamed chard or Romanesco broccoli and a cavernous glass of something red from Bordeaux.

A stew for deepest winter

for the stew

1.5kg stewing steak, chopped
   into 2.5cm pieces
50g seasoned plain flour
75g beef dripping
200g streaky bacon, chopped
   chunky
16 shallots, peeled
4 carrots, chopped
2 parsnips, chopped
4 sticks celery, chopped
900ml dark brown beer (such as
   Newcastle Brown Ale)
50g black treacle
8 anchovies, sliced
150g chestnut mushrooms, each
   cut in half
150g pickled walnuts, chopped
salt and pepper
600ml beef stock
handful each of thyme, sage
   and oregano, loosely tied

for the dumplings

350g plain flour
1 teaspoon baking powder
salt and pepper
2–3 tablespoons cold water
200g beef suet
2 teaspoons fresh horse radish,
   grated

a feast to serve a houseful of 8–10

I had this at my brother-in-law Simon's house in Devon, last Christmas, and Dad really loved it. Simon is a generous cook and frequently cooks up a Sunday storm in his beast of a range. He likes BIG-style cooking in the vein of Hugh Fearnley-Whittingstall and Jamie Oliver and Simon casts fistfuls of thyme into the stew, which reminds me of storm debris on the beach. The flotsam and jetsam of the stew are, in fact, pickled walnuts and winter root vegetables, entangled in the web of fragrant bouquet garni.

Rub the beef pieces into the flour seasoned with salt and pepper. Over a medium heat, in a large, heavy-based ovenproof pan, heat all of the beef dripping apart from 1 tablespoon, and brown-off the beef. Remove the meat from the pan and set aside.

Preheat the oven to 160°C/gas mark 3. Put the remaining tablespoon of beef dripping into the pan and fry the bacon over a medium heat until it softens.

Add the shallots to the pan, allowing them to colour ever so slightly. Next add the carrots, parsnips and celery. Stir together, then pour in the beer. Bring to a simmer, then add the black treacle, anchovies, chestnut mushrooms, pickled walnuts and seasoning. Add the stock and place the bunches of herbs ceremoniously on top. Bring back to a simmer, put the lid on and cook in the oven for 2½–3 hours. Half an hour before the end of cooking, make the dumplings.

Mix the dumpling ingredients with 2–3 tablespoons of cold water until the mixture comes together as a moist dough. Form into golf ball-sized dumplings and place on the top of the stew. Cook for 30 minutes.

Dad has always enjoyed a gadget or two to complement any activity he undertakes, a gadget for his camera, computer or, more recently, his kitchen. A space-age halogen cooker is the latest addition, which he uses to cook a roast chicken to perfection. These days, he always has a kitchen timer on the go when he phones. If it's 5pm he'll sign off with an 'I've got to go now, the timer's up!'

Roast chicken with herb salt and sage puddings

50g butter

1 free-range organic chicken, weighing 1.5–2kg (leave at room temperature for at least an hour prior to cooking)

for the herb salt

3–4 heaped tablespoons each of fresh thyme, oregano and rosemary

2 tablespoons salt

for 12 small sage puddings

12 teaspoons sunflower oil

25g plain four

2 egg yolks

300ml milk, warmed

12 sage leaves

serves 5–6

The skin on this roast chicken is sublime: a herby, salty, buttery crust that retains most of its greenness in cooking. You don't need to use all of the herb salt on the chicken if you don't want to – it will keep for a few days in an airtight jar, and you can enjoy using it to spruce up pizzas and pies, or make a herby salad dressing by adding oil, vinegar and garlic.

The sage puddings evolved from a culinary disaster, in which I had erroneously taken down batter-ingredient quantities and had ended up with a heavy batter. I salvaged this, even with its sugar content intact, to try out batter puddings for roast chicken, each topped with a fresh sage leaf. They were greedily gobbled up, so I'll be making them again.

Use the finest chicken, preferably organic and free-range, that you can afford. Aim high and try to get a bird from a local food producer, the kind that gets the 'freeze frame' treatment in current cookery shows, in the style of Grant Wood's iconic double portrait, *American Gothic* (1930), of a rural nineteenth-century American country couple, with pitchfork in hand.

This meal is great served with dauphinoise potatoes or a sweet potato gratin and fresh carrots, or even a crunchy salad with some beet stalks glinting through.

Chop the fresh herbs finely (I use a mezzaluna for this) and mix with the sea salt in a small jar. Preheat the oven to 200°C/gas mark 6.

Rub butter all over the breast and legs of the chicken and pat the herb salt onto the skin and into the cavity. Cook the chicken in the oven for 10 minutes, then reduce the oven temperature to 180°C/gas mark 4 and cook for a further 50–60 minutes. It is worth testing

the chicken after an hour of cooking by inserting a skewer into the deepest part of the leg. If the juices from here run clear, then it's done and can be taken out to rest (under some foil for 15 minutes).

Halfway through the chicken's cooking time, put a teaspoon of sunflower oil in each hole of a shallow muffin tin and put in the oven for 10 minutes to heat up. If you can arrange the oven so that the chicken is under the muffin tin at this stage, then so much the better. In a mixing bowl, mix the flour with the egg yolks, then add the warm milk in a constant stream, mixing until the batter is lump-free. Half fill each muffin hole with the thick batter and place a sage leaf on the top of each. Bake for 25–30 minutes, until golden and modestly puffed. (Try to time it so that you put the pudding batter into the oven when the chicken has been cooking for about 45 minutes, so they are ready simultaneously.)

Cream of ambrosia: orange and vanilla rice pudding

120g pudding rice
60g caster sugar
seeds of 1 vanilla pod
500ml double cream
500ml full fat milk
grated zest of 1 orange

enough for 4–5

Rice is such a brilliant template for any flavour fix you care to try. The basic mixture can be made more Moorish, both greedily and geographically speaking, by adding rosewater and pistachios, as Claudia Roden does. I love the low-level citrus and vanilla combination in this dish, the orange zest just about cutting through the mellow sweet cream and vanilla. If nectar was the beverage of choice for the Gods, then this was their food.

Preheat the oven 150°C/gas mark 2.

Pour everything into a shallow pudding basin, give it a gentle stir and cook for 2½ hours in the oven. The pudding should still have a small amount of liquid when it's done.

I now live in a beach house in South Devon with my three young children, Raz, Beren and Magi, and husband Diggory. We are lucky that the area in which we live has the highest concentration of organic-food producers in the UK. My friends Tom and Rachael from Old Cumming Organic Farm are a living part of that statistic. They grow the most magical salad leaves studded with rose petals and nasturtiums in a lush valley in South Devon. We regularly munch on these and other Devon goodies, including chilli chocolate, from the South Devon Chilli Farm in Loddiswell.

Dad lives on the north coast of Cornwall, about two hours drive from me. These days, it is sometimes him who suggests to me that I make a home-made soup to perk up one of my children if they are unwell and off school. We exchange tips about which purchases might freeze well, where to get the best mince pies and which are the latest superfoods.

Dad has since discovered, all by himself, a local farm shop on the edge of Dartmoor that provides him with much of his meat, all of his vegetables and weekly sweet treats. I might not have quite got him up to speed with the last 60 years of culinary evolution, or turned him into a galloping gourmet, but I've fed back to him a little bit of our family cookbook, whose simple recipes he can savour again and again.

At the turn of the last century my great grandfather built a farmhouse, in a colonial style, on top of a windy hill at Thurlibeer in North Cornwall. This was on the site of a former manor house mentioned in the Domesday Book of 1086 and described as a typical Cornish squire's manor, built of slate and granite. I never met my great grandfather, or my great grandmother, who came down to the West Country from London, and was said by those who still remember her to have brought beautiful clothes and quality furniture for her new life in the country.

I have a highly polished chair and a Victorian travel trunk of the grand tour era, stamped with her initials 'C.H.' for Carrie Harris. They had nine children, of which my grandfather was one.

Paul, as he was known (although the Christian names of Edward and Amos came first), took on the family farm, eventually buying out the shares of his siblings. His growing entrepreneurial spirit led him to start lending money to local people so that they could buy

Well-loved food
food from family and friends... Cornwall to Helsinki

their own homes in the post-war era, before it was commonplace for high-street banks to provide mortgages. My grandmother and he looked after evacuees during the War, some of whom we met recently when they came to revisit the area. The produce of their land, topped up by weekly visits from various grocery sellers, enabled my grandparents to be pretty much self-sufficient. I have been told that my grandparents' house was the place to see the Queen's Coronation, as they were one of the few families to own their own television set at that time. I think they had about 50 people in their living room that day in 1953. My mother and her sister and brother grew up in that farmhouse, and my brother and I always used to go and stay there during school holidays. Before the kettle had even been placed on the Rayburn for my parents' first holiday cup of tea, my brother and I would sneak into the dairy. With its long, cool slate counter tops, we slipped off the cake tin lids, one by one, and eyeballed the contents, to make sure we wouldn't lose out to the adults in the up-and-coming feasts. We always assumed this was an entirely covert operation and planned the order in which we would consume the contents of the tins.

You could see Widemouth Bay from the front lawn and fields, but we spent most of our time down at the beach. In the afternoons my brother and I would return for a daily feast, having swum in the salty lido in summer or, in winter, run the gauntlet of the Atlantic-blown waves smashing onto the concrete wall around the edge of the pool. We would wash the sand off our feet outside the back door, and walk into the kitchen to warm in front of the Rayburn, then cast our eyes over the tea-time spread that would be laid before us. Plates would be removed from the Rayburn piled high with warm savoury pies and pasties. Golden runner-bean chutney in jars with waxed discs would jostle for table space with warm salty Cornish potatoes. Home-made clotted cream would be brought out from the dairy, still resplendent with its Victorian food-safe, to go with slices of apple pie.

The scene was straight out of the '50s, although it was Cornwall in the '70s and '80s. My grandma would dress for afternoon tea, in the pleated and belted dresses of her youth. She was a traditional and prolific baker – on a Wednesday – and cooked Victoria sponges, currant buns, cheesecakes, saffron cakes, chocolate and cream roulades, jam tarts, bacon and egg pies, pasties and berry crumbles... and also made her own clotted cream, which was scolded in a shallow enamel dish. My grandmother still reminisces about Baking Wednesday and laments how she can no longer 'do' Christmas.

My mother's cooking in my childhood was a combination of traditional Cornish food passed down from my grandma, mixed with new recipes that she discovered in books and magazines during the '70s and '80s: lasagne, moussaka and something she called Danish Apple Charlotte (see page 31), a layered trifle of stewed apple, cream and gritty caramelised brown breadcrumbs. On Sundays we had a roast followed by a self-saucing Chocolate Fudge pudding from *The Times Cookery Book*. During the week we ate Cranks-inspired creations: rice salad with red peppers and pineapple, and pizza with a variety of experimental bases such as scone, whole-wheat bread and even potato. It was a time of trying exciting combinations of exotic foods that had been kindly flown in for us – and the further afield they came from, the better. It was air miles in reverse.

The historical tendency to stick two fingers up at the way your parents lived and go back to the values of your grandparents tends to be spot on. Keeping it local could not be truer of my grandparents' generation. Like my grandma, I cook local and mainly organic food. She would have donned her cream, pointy, calf-length wellies and picked the carrots and potatoes for lunch from her vegetable garden in the morning, whereas I go to my local farm shop and prod the soil-encrusted produce. Her meat came from the cows and sheep that grazed beneath the kitchen window in fields battered by salty sea air. For pork, she swapped beef. She didn't have access to strawberries in January, and I choose not to buy them at this time. My grandfather and his closest farming neighbour are now buried next to each other in an ancient Cornish churchyard. The neighbour's headstone reads that he farmed his land for '60 years'. My grandad, Amos, who died a few years later, trumped that, monumentally speaking, with '70 years'!

Bacon and egg pie

250g shortcrust pastry, made
    using 180g plain flour and
    90g cold unsalted butter

for the filling
3 tablespoons olive oil
2 large red onions
1 tablespoon sugar
400g back bacon or pancetta,
    chopped
6 eggs
salt and pepper
50g pine nuts
handful of flat-leaf parsley, torn

serves 6–8

This recipe is from my Cornish grandmother's kitchen. Before she downsized from her farmhouse to the local village about ten years ago, she would change into a '50s shift dress at about half-past three and lay the table with savoury pies, sliced pasties, trifles and more.

In this recipe I tend to use red onions, to echo the puce pink of the bacon, although I'm sure my grandma would have used the brown ones from her very own vegetable garden in full view of the kitchen window.

Make the pastry (see page 8 for method), wrap in clingfilm and leave in the fridge for 20 minutes.

Preheat the oven to 180°C/gas mark 4 and start making the filling. Heat the olive oil in a large thick-based pan over a moderate heat. Add the chopped onion and soft brown sugar and cook, stirring, for about 10 minutes. Then add the chopped bacon and cook for another 5 minutes until things have softened. The bacon needs to maintain a juicy pink colour, and not become crispy.

While the filling is cooking, whisk the eggs in a jug and season well with salt and pepper. Set this aside for the moment.

Remove the pastry from the fridge and roll it out to fit a 30cm tart tin. Bake blind for 15–20 minutes, until the pastry is lightly coloured and dry. Turn the oven down to 170°C/gas mark 3.

Arrange the bacon-and-onion mixture on the base of the pie case, then pour over the seasoned egg mixture. Sprinkle with fresh torn parsley and pine nuts. Cook for 35–40 minutes until the tart is golden brown and feels firm in the centre.

Rococo trifle

for the meringue
5 egg whites
300g caster sugar

for the custard
5 egg yolks
40g sugar
500ml double cream
1 vanilla pod, split, with seeds
    removed and retained

for the fruit layer
200g Savoiardi biscuits (or use
    the same quantity of vanilla
    genoise or madeira cake, cut
    into pieces)
500g fresh raspberries or frozen
    mixed berries
50g caster sugar
2 tablespoons orange flower
    water

for the cream layer
200g mascarpone
200ml double cream

for the topping
100g fresh raspberries
icing sugar

makes enough for a family

I have been making this for the last ten years and always feel a warm appreciative glow when I bring it out. It does a turn at big family get-togethers, and within my immediate family it is rather egotistically referred to as *my* trifle. In having to think of a slightly more modest and accurate nomenclature, 'Rococo' seems to aptly sum up its calorific and visual excesses. It's so beautiful, it reminds me of incredible, semelparous flowers that, by definition, flower once in a lifetime, then theatrically die.

The concept of using meringue as a kind of crunchy duvet came from Nigella's passion-fruit trifle in *How to be a Domestic Goddess*. Once I had worked out the top layer, I then moved to the bottom. For the first layer I was content enough with a mix of red berries (raspberries and blackberries) sloshed with some fragrant orange-flower water and a sprinkling of sugar, plus slices of cake or Savoiardi biscuits. Heavily and heavenly vanilla-speckled custard became the next, using the yolks left over from the meringue (don't say I'm not frugal). Then a layer of cream (in fact, a mix of mascarpone and double cream – to lighten!) combined with half of the broken meringue. This was finally topped by the rest of the meringue, and sprinkled with fresh raspberries and a dusting of icing sugar; it is surely my *Gesamtkunstwerk*.

Normally I am of the Bauhaus opinion – in cooking, and in life in general – that less is more. But just not here.

Preheat the oven to 140°C /gas mark 1.

First make the meringue by whisking the egg whites to stiff peaks, then slowly folding in the sugar. Spread the mixture 2.5cm deep onto a baking sheet lined with parchment paper. Bake in the oven for about 40 minutes. Remove and, when cool, break the meringue into shards and set aside.

Next make the custard (or you could use a shop-bought good-quality vanilla custard here – they come in 500ml tubs). Heat the cream in a wide pan with the vanilla seeds and the split vanilla pod until nearly boiling, but not quite. Meanwhile, mix the egg yolks and sugar together in a bowl, then whisk in the hot cream mixture, taking out the vanilla pod just before you do so. Pour the whole mixture back into the pan. (Some say you should wash the pan first. I never do, and always get away with it.) Stir until the liquid thickens. At the slightest look of it curdling, plunge into a sink of very cold water and stir frantically – it really works.

To assemble the trifle, first place the cake pieces or Savoiardi biscuits in the base of a large serving bowl. Add the fruit, sugar and 2 tablespoons of orange flower water, and give it all a very gentle stir. Now spread the custard layer on top. In a separate bowl, beat the two creams together and stir in half of the crushed meringue pieces. Spread this over the custard layer, then sprinkle with the remaining meringue-bergs and fresh raspberries. Dust with icing sugar and bring out to rapturous applause.

During the '70s mum started to experiment with the international cuisines that were being promoted on the radio and telly. Like lots of British families, and perhaps being more insecure then than we are now about our culinary heritage, we were quick to jump from steak-and-kidney pie to spaghetti bolognese, or from jam roly-poly to Black Forest Gateau. Mum's fabulous 'international' dessert, Danish Apple Charlotte, was a post-roast favourite.

Mum's Danish apple charlotte

100g butter, melted

100g white breadcrumbs (use about 3 slices of bread)

50g light muscovado sugar

6 large apples (about 750g), such as Bramleys, peeled, cored and chopped into mouth-sized pieces

100g caster sugar

1 tablespoon elderflower cordial

1 tablespoon water

300ml whipping cream (a 284ml tub will do)

serves 4–5

I'm not sure from where my mum got this recipe (probably from her favourite cookery book of the time, Katie Stewart's *The Times Cookery Book*), but it became a regular family favourite – normally after roast chicken on a Sunday.

As a child I don't think I ever really believed there was anything Danish about it. I presumed that in '70s Britain most people weren't intimately familiar with Danish cuisine, so Ms Stewart wouldn't have to defend her cross-cultural nomenclature, but in this modern world of Google-mania it seems Ms Stewart's recipe did indeed have genuine Danish provenance. Danish Apple Charlotte, with its relished breadcrumbs and cream, abounds in cyberspace. For me, crisp, caramelised breadcrumbs and cream are like a hit of concentrated nostalgia, but don't be tempted to add extra cream, as I once did. Thinish layers, that leave you wanting, are what it's all about.

Preheat the oven to 180°C/gas mark 4. Melt the butter in a frying pan. When it bubbles, add the breadcrumbs and the muscovado sugar and stir to coat the crumbs. Continue until the crumbs are crisp, then set to one side to cool down completely.

In a large pan set over a low-to-moderate heat, stew the apple with the caster sugar, elderflower cordial and water for about 7 minutes, until the apple is soft at the edges, but retains a sense of form in the middle. Take off the heat and allow to cool. Whip the cream to soft mounds.

To assemble – it looks good in a glass bowl – first add a layer of apple, then whipped cream, then caramelised breadcrumbs; keep going until all the ingredients are used and finish with breadcrumbs.

In my teens, alongside learning my set text of *Pride and Prejudice,* I would read Nigella Lawson's reviews in *Vogue* of restaurants such as the Walnut Tree in Abergavenny, The Hole in the Wall in Bath, Sally Clarke's in Notting Hill and frequently Alice Water's Chez Panisse in Berkeley, San Francisco. I should have been learning about the oxygen cycle for my up-and-coming exams. I wasn't going to have the means to be a client at these establishments, let alone be able to get to them, for a long, long time, but that didn't dampen my appetite for discovering far-flung culinary delights from the comfort of my bedroom, on the glossy page. Back in the real kitchen, downstairs, a wholefood revolution was going on.

I felt quite emotional recently when I opened our family Cranks cookbook (*The Cranks Recipe Book*). It was the well-thumbed one that mum would have used to select her meals – its yellowing pages are reassuringly splattered with traces of oil and butter. I still love looking at those centre spreads with their stoneware bowls and great hunks of bread – the subliminal message being that we can eat our way into a healthier and better life, and feel good about it, even if we are living the yuppie dream.

Because my mother had grown up living the *real* good life, my parents didn't aspire to a kind of Tom-and-Barbara suburban 'semi-sufficiency'. Being one generation removed from the real country, however, I would have loved it. As it was, I had to make do with the rustic chic that my friends, the Evans (whose family set up the wholefood chain Cranks) embraced at their house. Huge, scrubbed-pine refectory tables held a seemingly endless supply of wholemeal bread, great slabs of Quickes cheddar and thick natural yogurt.

Cranks-style sunflower bread

450g wholemeal flour

1 teaspoon salt

7g sachet dried yeast (about 2 teaspoons)

3 tablespoons good runny honey (preferably locally sourced)

300–400ml water

100g sunflower seeds

makes 2 x ½lb loaves

I have never had my DNA taken and tested. But I imagine there would be a strand, possibly highlighted in an earthy brown hue, that would be labelled 'Sunflower loaf'. I've eaten so much of this over the years and continue to do so with my children.

At a recent school reunion, a friend reminded me of a time when I used to bake a loaf of this bread in Devon, then deliver it to her in London as a present. On the return trip I would bring back tubs of Ben and Jerry's ice cream.

My school friend Catrin Evans is the granddaughter of the '60s founders of Cranks, Kay and David Canter. I remember her beautiful rustic kitchen in the '80s as always having a couple of

fresh sunflower loaves on the bread board, with a knife ready, implying that any guest could casually help themselves to the next slice. I think this was one of my early definitions of luxury, later challenged by the box of Alphonso mangoes to be found on the floor of a friend's family kitchen in the Sydney suburbs for picking at during the day.

This loaf has an inherent moistness, which comes from the hydroscopic properties of honey.

If using a bread maker, follow the manufacturer's instructions regarding the order of ingredients; set to 'medium' size and choose the colour of crust you prefer.

Otherwise, put all of the dry ingredients (leaving about a tablespoon of the sunflower seeds for finishing) in a large mixing bowl. Mix the honey into the water and add to the dry ingredients to form a dough. Knead the dough for about 10 minutes.

Divide the dough into two and put each half into a 225g (½lb) loaf tin. Finish with a sprinkling of sunflower seeds on top. Let the dough prove in a warm place until it has risen sufficiently; it won't double like lighter white loaves, but it should stand proud above the edge of the tin. Preheat the oven to 200°C/gas mark 6.

Bake in the oven for 35–40 minutes. When cooked, the base of the bread should have a hollow sound when tapped.

Whole-wheat shortbread

150g wholemeal flour
100g butter, very soft
100g raw brown sugar
2 teaspoons golden caster sugar
 for sprinkling

makes about 15 slices

To me, this recipe says austerity in a time of '80s excess. It has a slightly gritty but pleasant feel in the mouth and is a sensible solution for the afternoon sugar slump.

I have tinkered with the original '80s recipe here and revved up the butter a notch (following family complaints the first time around). In the war years, when butter was rationed, margarine would have been used in baking. It came in a white block with an accompanying pack of yellow dye (made from extract of carrot) that was stirred in to contrive a butterly appearance. So the extra butter is definitely to be relished in this minimalist context.

Preheat the oven to 160°C/gas mark 3. Line a 25cm x 25cm square cake tin or brownie tin with baking parchment.

Pulse all of the ingredients together in a food processor. (Alternatively rub the flour and butter together in a mixing bowl, then add the sugar.)

Put the mixture into the prepared tin and pat it down with the back of a wooden spoon. Incise 15 finger-shaped slices, then bake for 20–25 minutes. Sprinkle with caster sugar and cool on a wire rack.

Novelli's lemsip

juice of ½ unwaxed, organic
   lemon
1 teaspoon runny honey
capful of Cointreau
boiling water

enough for 1 mugful

Less a recipe – more a reminder – of a lovely drink and a lovely moment. The perfect pick-me-up for a real, or even fantasy, cold.

I used to cycle to work at Keith Floyd's restaurant all year round. In the winter I arrived bedraggled, often with nose streaming, to be rescued by our new young Head Chef, Jean-Christophe Novelli with his patriotic version of lemsip. *Mais oui.* In retrospect, you can probably appreciate that my snuffles lingered on for much longer than could be reasonably accounted for.

I actually made myself a cup of this whilst writing this book. Using an organic unwaxed lemon and eucalyptus honey from the French market that visits Kingsbridge, the drink itself is even good enough to have a fantasy cold for, since I no longer have JCN on hand.

Please use organic unwaxed lemons. A friend of mine who had worked on an Israeli kibbutz described to me the ritual waxing of the apples and lemons prior to their despatch to Europe. A veneer of tacky varnish gets hand-painted onto the fruit before they are frozen for a year prior to their arrival in our shops.

Pour the lemon juice, honey and Cointreau into your chosen cup. Top up with freshly boiled water. Enjoy the warm glow as it slips down your throat.

... to Helsinki

The current male line of my generation have been seduced by Scandinavia, my brother marrying into a Finnish family and my cousin into a Swedish one. Some of our favourite times as a family have been at a lakeside summerhouse in southern Finland. We drive up north from our home on the south coast of England to Newcastle, take the North Sea ferry, which kisses the coast of Norway, watch the jellyfish in the harbour at Kristiansand and see the nuclear submarine pop up next to the plimsoll line. We drive a straight line across Sweden, under the old coal-mining cable cars in the centre, and eventually settle into the mini-city that exists on the many-storied Viking Line ship in the port at Stockholm. This skirts the Baltic, then weaves through the archipelago of islands, first the Swedish, then, seamlessly, the Finnish. The islands that nestle around Stockholm contain jewel-like, yellow-umber summerhouses, over which the ferry, with its vast, vertical profile, casts a temporary shadow. I have woken in the middle of the night as the ferry judders up to the jetty at the midway island of Fasta Åland. Officially Finnish, it has a closer working allegiance to Sweden, so the islanders speak Swedish. You never really break into the open sea, and you have a feeling of being looked after and protected by these islands all the way to Finland. On the morning of arrival, the Baltic is oily calm, dotted with rocky outcrops and scraggy islands with stunted spruce trees.

We have all fallen for the summerhouse culture of Finland: the indulgence of spending a whole day in and out of the traditional wood-fired sauna, running down the wooden jetty and jumping in the lake, leaping back into the sauna. On a huge lakeside griddle we cook sweet waffles in an antique, heart-shaped waffle iron. We aspire to be colourfully dressed in head-to-toe Marimekko like the locals. At dusk the children lap up the Moomin stories and, just for the thrill of it, crazy adults (myself very much included) go elk watching.

There is a quiet reverence for collecting and preserving your own berries in Finland – Finns are zealous about gathering and freezing berries in the same way that the French and Italians go mad for funghi. If you are lucky enough to see the inside of a Finn's freezer you will also simultaneously see them smugly glowing with pride, in much the same way that we might if we have a full tank of oil, or a tall stack of logs, before the winter price hikes. Much of our time, when not in the sauna, is spent collecting berries. We collect them from swamps (cloudberries), forest tracks (wild raspberries and lingonberries – these latter are also called cowberries, foxberries and partridge berries) and the ground (blueberries), and gorge on moreish cardamom buns called Korvapuusti.

In the summer, the edge of my sister-in-law's garden in Naantali, southwest Finland, dissolves into a carpet of blueberries. They crawl across the forest floor, the plants entangled. You cannot avoid treading on them and feel guilty about the trail of berry carnage left in your wake. These wild forest berries have a tarter and tangier flavour than their cultivated cousins.

Cloudberry cookies

115g butter
55g golden caster sugar
125g plain flour
1 egg, separated, both yolk and
   white beaten
50g walnuts , chopped
cloudberry jam (see page 186
   for suppliers)

enough for about 12 cookies

To the uninitiated, a cloudberry might seem a whimsical fruit to be picked from the cloud forest. Or perhaps it is a made-up berry from a Moomin story, something Moomin Mama might have to search the forest for, past the ghost-shaped Hattifatners and avoiding the icy breath of The Groke. In fact it grows in swamps, bogs and marshes and rather romantically ripens under the 24-hour midnight sun. I can only think that cloudberries are so-called because the watery meadows where they grow reflect the skies in all their miraculous formations.

Cloudberries ('lakka') are an Arctic delicacy of Finland, Sweden and Norway and used to be known as 'Arctic gold' because small farmers could boost their incomes by selling them at the manor houses of the iron-ore mine owners. Prices have reached 10 Euros per kilo, although unfortunately this year's cloudberry harvest was small due to the cold nights in early summer.

This recipe comes from Tillmans, the Swedish sellers of organic fruit saft (cordial) and cloudberry jam. These delicious cookies, with their luminous puddle of cloudberry jam, provide a self-referential ending for the berry, as it reflects the sky once again, but this time from the cookie.

Preheat the oven to 150°C/gas mark 2. Cream the butter and sugar together in a mixing bowl. Add the egg yolk and flour and mix well until a dough forms. Roll the dough into 12 small balls and dip them in the egg white, then roll them in the chopped walnuts.

Place the balls of dough on a baking sheet. Press down the centres gently with your thumb to make a small depression in each.

Bake for 5 minutes, then press the centres again to reform. Bake for another 10–15 minutes. While they're still warm, fill the centres with jam.

A bowl of porridge with blueberries

porridge oats, 45g per person
water, 100ml per person
milk, 210ml per person
pinch of salt
blueberries, a small handful,
    per person
runny honey or agave nectar

This would be my breakfast of choice everyday, if I could get a regular supply of organic blueberries – an uncomplicated taste of Moomin valley.

I now make porridge the Finnish way, using a balloon whisk instead of a wooden spoon, to get an easy, even texture. Mix the oats with the water, milk and a pinch of salt in a saucepan. Over a moderate heat, bring the porridge to the boil and simmer for about 6 minutes, whisking slowly and gently every now and again. Spoon into warm bowls and scatter with blueberries and a lateral drizzling of a good runny honey or agave nectar.

Amy and the wolf biscuits

125g icing sugar
½ teaspoon vanilla extract
1 egg yolk
250g butter, softened
370g plain flour, plus extra for
    dusting
pinch of fine salt
100g dark chocolate, melted

makes about 25–30 biscuits,
depending on shape and size

'Long, long ago, far, far away. There was a girl who had to save. Her mother's sick, lying in bed. Risked her own life, for someone else instead…' My brother Dexter writes contemporary children's music in Finland. I recently adapted one of his first musicals, called *Amy and the Wolf*, into a puppet musical at my children's school, and made these girl and wolf-shaped biscuits for the interval refreshments.

The market place for interesting cookie cutters has grown hugely. My fledgling collection includes; a Moomin family, elk, snail, hedgehog, reindeer… online, I've got my eye on some new cutters: a cactus, a Harry Potter 'sorting hat' and a unicorn.

Preheat the oven to 200°C/gas mark 6. Mix together the icing sugar, vanilla extract, egg yolk and butter in a bowl. Add the flour and salt and mix to a firm dough. Form into a flat slab, wrap in clingfilm and rest in the fridge for about an hour.

Lightly dust a counter top with flour, then roll out the dough to 5mm thick. Cut out biscuits with cookie cutters, place them on a baking sheet lined with parchment and bake for 8–10 minutes or so, checking from 8 minutes onwards. They should have a golden edge, but remain relatively pale and soft in the centre. Move gently to a wire rack to cool. Finally decorate with melted chocolate.

Swedish berry crumble with vanilla cream

for the filling
500g berries, fresh or frozen
1 tablespoon caster sugar

for the topping
50g caster sugar
100g butter, cold, cubed
150g plain flour

for the vanilla cream
seeds of 1 vanilla pod
250ml thick double cream
2 teaspoons icing sugar

serves 4–6

Normally the question in our home is 'would you like a bit of fruit with your crumble?' as we pile on oversized spoonfuls with extra crumble topping. This delicate Swedish version, a *smulpaj*, doesn't have a thick British wodge of crumble as a topping – it has more of a lacy crumble, both veiling and concealing the berry swamp beneath. The billowing clouds of vanilla cream, so Scandi, make this a lighter option than its British cousin.

Preheat the oven to 200°C/gas mark 6. Scatter the berries into a shallow ovenproof dish and sprinkle over the caster sugar. (The dish only needs to be about 1cm deep at most; I use a white ceramic one that is about 20cm x 20cm.) Set aside.

Combine the topping ingredients in a food processor (or in a mixing bowl) and pulse (or rub) until the mixture forms a rubbly crumble. Scatter the crumble mixture over the fruit, allowing tantalizing glimpses of fruit to show through in places. Bake in the oven for 25–35 minutes.

While the crumble is cooking, make the vanilla cream by stirring the vanilla and sugar into the cream and whisking to slightly aerate. Unless the kitchen is obscenely hot, I keep this on the counter until needed, to allow the vanilla to infuse the cream. Serve with the crumble; don't be mean with the vanilla cream. Is that my first rhyming couplet, or the beginning of a rap?

Over the years, my sister-in-law's summerhouse (*mökki* in Finnish) has become a cluster of small wooden buildings. The original house, built in 1965 by Leena's father Jouni and her grandfather, has a veranda with a white swinging chair, one L-shaped room containing a stove, a dresser for crockery, a table, and bunk beds that hug the warm brick wall of the wood-fired sauna on the other side. There is an adjoining workshop and wood store. A newer 'guest' house has been built slightly behind and uphill of the original. The compost loo sits in its own pitched-roof building; a bowl filled with well-water stands on a wash-stand and a linen hand towel hangs outside under the spruce trees. This was one of the last summerhouses in the area to adopt electricity. The lamps are still oil powered and we often use candles. Even now the solar panel is connected to a solitary socket used mainly for charging mobile phones and digital camera batteries!

Drinking water is collected further along the track, past the summerhouse next door and beyond the one with an extended family of ladybird-painted river stones protecting the entrance. The house next door is a seductive, distressed wreck in Farrow & Ball's finest, whose owners are being offered unheard-of Euros from the *nouveau* Russian *riche* (Russia is only a three-hour drive away on this perimeter of Europe-past). For the sauna, water to fill the tin hot-water cylinder is collected in bucketfuls from the lake at the bottom of the garden and is heated over a wood fire surrounded by blackened brick walls. We sauna, then hot-foot it down the jetty and into the lake, swim around a flat grey rock and repeat until thoroughly relaxed. A double-sided swinging seat with a roof is a recent addition. We also have an area enclosed by logs where we sit and cook at a huge smooth griddle, like a giant steel drum. My brother takes the children and Ukko the retriever across the lake to the swamp where they hunt for elusive cloudberries.

A small, chalky white-painted rowing boat is gently tethered to the jetty that reaches out from the rough grass of the garden. The first time I went fishing in the lake, we were ill-prepared for me casting out and hooking a pike so long and ferocious it would have taken out my toes if we had hauled it into the boat. Besides, it would not have fitted into the yellow bucket we had brought for the purpose.

Swedish crayfish and rice

250g long-grain rice (white
    or brown)
25g butter
2 shallots, finely chopped
2 cloves garlic, crushed
250ml white wine
500ml double cream
750g crayfish tails, cooked
3–4 heaped tablespoons fresh
    dill, chopped
salt and pepper
1–2 lemons

serves 4–5 comfortably

The Swedish crayfish-fest of Kräftskiva celebrates the traditional opening of the crayfish season in Sweden. Crayfish is cooked with crown dill, the flowering head of the herb, eaten alongside Västerbotten cheese and accompanied by Akvavit and other kinds of snaps. People wear paper hats and the drinking games go on into the small hours.

We missed out on Kräftskiva, by a day or so, when we were last in Sweden, but we did get treated to this dress rehearsal in the form of a mellow, creamy, crayfish stew and rice. It's difficult to get raw crayfish in the UK, but you can use pre-cooked tails, like the Swedes do. If you do manage to get some raw ones, or fish for your own, then give them a little longer in the pot than is suggested below.

The allure of the summer, when there is so much darkness bookending the year, is apparent in the way that the Finns inhale every droplet of the season, with food that sings of the south: citrus blossom, watermelon and fragile salad leaves.

Cook the rice (to go alongside the crayfish stew) in double its volume of cold water. I think this is an old Delia-ism, and it works for me every time. You boil the rice for about 12 minutes – there should be no water left, but if there is, switch off the heat anyway and cover with a tea towel and that will absorb the remaining water.

In a large pan, heat the butter and gently fry the shallots with the garlic on a low heat for about 5–7 minutes until they have softened. Increase the heat to moderate, add the wine and cook for about 5 minutes until it has reduced slightly. Turn the heat down to low again and add the cream, stirring everything through. Cook for 7–8 minutes. Add the crayfish tails and dill, season, and cook for a further 3–4 minutes. Squeeze in lemon juice to taste.

Serve on top of the warm white rice, so that it trickles down through the swollen gains, like rainwater in limestone. Apparently, it's pretty much obligatory to eat this alongside a glass of vodka or beer.

Dill hotcakes with kiln-roast salmon

250g kiln-roast salmon

for the hotcakes
250g ricotta, at room
   temperature
170ml milk
4 eggs, separated
150g plain flour
pinch of salt
1 teaspoon baking powder
1 heaped tablespoon fresh dill,
   chopped
50g butter

for the dill dressing
1 heaped tablespoon fresh dill,
   chopped
juice and grated zest of
   ½ lemon
500ml sour cream
salt and pepper

makes about 10 hotcakes

On our first Scandinavian road trip, we ate the freshest kiln-roast salmon at a restaurant perched by Lake Vänern in Sweden. The area is also famous for its pike, some whose heads live on, long after their bodies have been devoured, in artful stuffed and varnished displays.

To make the dressing, mix the fresh dill, the lemon juice and the lemon zest into the sour cream. Add salt and pepper, moderating to individual taste. Put the dressing to one side while you make the hotcakes.

In a large mixing bowl, whisk the ricotta until lump-free, then incorporate the milk and egg yolks. Sift the flour, salt and baking powder together into the mixing bowl, whisking as you go. In a separate bowl, whisk up the egg whites until foamy, then fold them into the ricotta mixture with the rest of the chopped dill.

Place a frying pan that has been wiped with butter (I use a piece of butter wrapper, kitchen roll, or a pastry brush for this) over a moderate heat. Fry the hotcakes, two at a time. Luckily, they have a tendency to form their own perfect circles (or ovals, depending on the quantity of mixture ladled in). They take about 2–3 minutes a side to cook.

It troubles me to say, 'plate up' in the manner of so many pseudo TV chefs, but that's exactly what you need to do at this point, in assembling the three elements. On each warm plate, place two hotcakes, a generous spoonful of dill sauce and some fat flakes of the kiln-roast salmon. The hotcakes will cry out for an accompanying glass of champers.

When I want to breathe some summerhouse oxygen and recapture the essence of summerhouse living, I immerse myself in *The Summer Book* by Tove Jansson. She wrote it in 1972, the year I was born, and the year after her own mother died. My mother gave me a copy of the book a year before she herself died. It has chapters entitled The Morning Swim, The Magic Forest, The Neighbour, Dead Calm and Playing Venice, in which the family make a wooden city sinking in a swamp. It also deals with the mortality and minutiae of the island's inhabitants, such as the incredible fragility of the

moss: 'Step on it once and it rises the next time it rains. The second time, it doesn't rise back up. And the third time you step on moss, it dies'.

Tove Jansson (1914–2001) is best known as the creator of the Moomin children's stories, those magic-forest tales of slightly hippo-like creatures: Moomin Mama with her stripy apron, the original domestic goddess; Moomin Papa with his black top hat; and also a female-gendered Snork Maiden, and the butterfly collecting Hemulen. Tove lived on Klovharun, a small island in the Gulf of Finland, where most of her books were written. *The Summer Book* was one of ten novels she wrote for adults. It is regarded as a modern classic throughout Scandinavia, where it has never been out of print. It is about an elderly artist and her six-year-old granddaughter who spend a summer together on a tiny island in the Gulf of Finland.

Summerhouse waffles

400g plain flour, sifted
100g caster sugar
2 teaspoons baking powder
pinch of fine salt
4 eggs
600ml milk
200g butter, melted and cooled

enough for 15–20 waffles

Cooked over an open fire and paired with a forest-berry jam and vanilla cream, these epitomize carefree Scandinavian holidays at the summerhouse. The family of my Finnish sister-in-law Leena has an exquisite 50-year-old cast iron waffle iron that was found in a local antique shop, and Jouni, her father, is indeed the family waffle-master. The flower-shaped pan cooks five heart-shaped waffles. I've tried to recapture the feel of *Swallows and Amazons*, or is it more *Lord of the Flies*, by having these at the end of a barbecue. It makes an unexpected diversion from the ubiquitous flame-roasted marshmallows.

Put all the dry ingredients (flour, sugar, baking powder and salt) into a large mixing bowl. Put all the wet ingredients (eggs, milk and melted butter) into another bowl and beat until the eggs and milk become one. Pour the wet mix into the centre of the dry mix and whisk until you have a smooth batter.

If using a waffle machine, follow the manufacturer's instructions. If making over an open fire, gently prewarm a lightly greased waffle iron. Pour some of the mixture into the pan, being careful not to slop it over the sides, and cook for about 5 minutes. When golden and cooked inside, tip the waffle out and serve with jam and whipped cream.

Summer in Finland is a time when all sorts of festivals take place: the world championships for sitting in the sauna, carrying wives, swamp soccer, ant-nest sitting, mobile-phone throwing and playing the air guitar at the Air Guitar World Championships in Oulu. My brother Dexter visited one of these traditional midsummer festivals recently, and is now the world-record holder for hurling the *vihta* (the bundle of birch sticks that are traditionally used in saunas) the furthest!

Juhannus, or midsummer, is celebrated throughout Scandinavia. The day is particularly significant in Finland where it is recognised as a national holiday. It is a time to be with friends and family and is usually celebrated with a big meal of pickled herring and smoked fish followed by the first strawberries of the year. After the meal everyone heads to parties and builds a *kokko*, a huge bonfire by the water that is a part of the old tradition of cleansing and warding off evil spirits.

Traditional midsummer foods were dairy products. After a long winter indoors cows once again started to produce more milk as they grazed the rich green summer fields. Nowadays dairy products are often replaced with grilled sausages (*makkara*), and new potatoes. Cloudberries are also quintessential summer fruits and stalls open up down by the harbour in Helsinki and in the car parks of supermarkets across the country.

Summer soup

1 tablespoon olive oil

8 spring onions, sliced

3 cloves garlic, crushed

2 celery stalks, finely chopped

3 peppers (mixture of yellow and red), sliced

4 carrots, finely chopped

handful of thyme sprigs

2 litres chicken stock or plain water

100g edamame or soya beans

150g penne, or other small pasta such as orechiette or ozo

serves 6–8

This is a vibrant summer soup in which the individual elements retain their texture. It's great for harvesting from the vegetable box or fridge shelf – and when you do, bear in mind that nutritionists are now telling us to eat all the colours of the rainbow. A bowl of this with some hand-torn sourdough bread would make me really happy on a summer's evening.

Heat the olive oil in a large, heavy-based pan and add the spring onions, garlic, celery and peppers. Sauté gently for about 10 minutes and then add the carrots and sprigs of thyme. Add the stock to the pan and bring to the boil.

Simmer for 10 minutes, until the carrots are tender, then add the edamame beans and pasta. Cook for a further 10 minutes until the pasta is cooked.

Finnish salad with orange blossom dressing

½ medium watermelon
½ cucumber, sliced into moons
750g (unshelled weight) broad
 beans
200g feta cheese

for the dressing
1 tablespoon orange blossom
 water
1 tablespoon white wine
 vinegar
3 tablespoons olive oil
salt and pepper

enough for 4–5 on the side

The Finns eat a large bowl of salad with pretty much any kind of meal, from cold tarts through to sizzling hot roasts and even Christmas dinner. They adore watermelon and feta cheese in their salads – a physical presence of southern foods for northern souls. On my first visit to a Finnish supermarket I was amazed to see the feta 'aisle'! It contained maybe 20 or 30 different kinds of feta from various countries.

This salad may well be served at the beginning of a Finnish feast, shortly after the portentous word *kippis* ('cheers', but try saying it out loud, at speed!) has been uttered. It needs to be served up quickly, otherwise the watermelon will give over its liquid to the bottom of the salad bowl and dilute the sunny dressing that goes with the salad. By the way, all alcohol above 4.7% proof must be purchased at the state-run liquor shops, appropriately called *Alko*.

My brother's summer holiday starts at the end of May and he returns to his job as a teacher in the second week of August. In the third week of August summer folds into autumn... a slight chill runs through the air and the Finnish autumn blows in.

Start with the watermelon, by cutting it in half and chopping the flesh into cubes. I never bother extracting the seeds, finding their gentle crunch a welcome contrast to the sweet yielding flesh (and, anyhow, the French eat the seeds alongside an aperitif).

Arrange the cubes in a shallow platter or bowl. Scatter over the sliced cucumber and broad beans, and crumble the feta over the salad (barrel-aged feta crumbles well). All of this needs to be done with a sense of urgency, as any ripe melon starts losing its juice with the first cut (or in my case, in the shopping bag).

Mix the dressing ingredients together in a small jug and spoon gently over the salad. A direct hit of salt and pepper on the melon works well, but also acts as a catalyst for drawing out more water from the melon, so go easy on the seasoning.

Korvapuusti

for the dough
250ml tepid milk
100g caster sugar
1 teaspoon salt
2 teaspoons ground cardamom
1 egg, lightly beaten
650g plain flour
7g sachet dried yeast (about
    2 teaspoons)
125g butter, softened

for the filling
80g butter, very soft
50g caster sugar
2 tablespoons ground cinnamon

for the topping
2–3 tablespoons pearl sugar
1 egg, lightly beaten

makes about 25 buns

Korvapuusti, which means 'slap on the ear' in Finnish and refers to the flattened-shape of the buns, has a liberal flow of butter, sugar and cinnamon at its centre and is imbued with mystical cardamom at its heart. Cinnamon is supposed to be good for circulation, which I suppose gives this cold-climate bun an added practical dimension. In Finland you can buy a ready-mixed sugar-and-cinnamon product called Kanelli-sokeri, but it's more than fine to mix your own.

On our first afternoon in Finland we normally arrive to a table laid with Korvapuusti, candles and coffee, which are enjoyed while sitting in the warm fug of the kitchen, created by buttery, cardamom-laced dough baking. You need really fresh ground cardamom. The Finns go through loads of the stuff in these beautiful semi-opaque capsules. I either get cardamom sent over to England, or bring it back myself and end up showing it to, and sniffing it with, the suspicious men at customs.

To make the dough, mix the milk, sugar, salt, cardamom and egg together in a large bowl. Add half of the flour, and the yeast, and stir into a soft dough. Mix the softened butter into the dough, then add as much from the rest of the flour as is needed – the dough is ready when it no longer sticks to the bowl or to your fingers. Cover the mixing bowl with a clean, dry tea towel and leave the dough to rise in a warm place for about 30 minutes.

Tip out the dough onto a floured board or counter top and knead for about 5 minutes. Halve the dough and roll out one part into a rectangular shape, approximately 1cm thick.

Now for the filling. Spread half the soft butter onto the dough, and sprinkle with half of both the sugar and cinnamon. Roll up the rectangle tightly, starting from the long side. Cut the log into even, triangular pieces with the back of a knife. Turn the pieces upwards and press down the centres of the Korvapuusti with your finger, so that the cut edges bulge out on both sides.

Repeat the process with the other half of the dough.

Place the Korvapuusti onto baking sheets lined with greaseproof paper and prove for 30 minutes. Afterwards, preheat the oven to 200°C/gas mark 6. Brush the buns with beaten egg and sprinkle with coarse sugar, such as pearl sugar. Bake on the middle shelf of the oven for approximately 10–15 minutes, until golden brown. Serve the Korvapuusti with a large cup of milky coffee.

I took a year out from my art-history degree in London to go travelling with Diggory. We started in chilly Moscow, where we had a friend who lived in an oak-panelled and tapestry-hung ex-KGB apartment, somewhere near the subway station of Biblioteka Imeni Lenina on the Sokolnicheskaya Line of the Moscow Metro. We moved through humid South East Asia, including Sumatra, which was the highlight.

We spent the night in a Batak house, eating Nasi Goren for supper and a fresh batch for breakfast. We were threateningly pelted with stones by some local teenagers, then took the slow boat to Java – me in a cabin for four, with eight Javanese women, and Digs in a cabin with three Dutch chaps. We wanted to travel the length of the whole Indonesian chain, through Bali, Lombok, Komodo, Flores and ultimately Timor (I'm amazed that I can still remember the order of the islands from west to east). Visiting East Timor would have been problematic because of the political situation, but we never had to face any potential threat as our funds ran dry and we took a flight from Jakarta to Sydney, just into the New Year.

Ozone inspired
tales from beach-side cooking

In Sydney

All of my passions were within easy reach on foot, by harbour ferry, bus, train or in our vintage buttercup-yellow, split-screen VW combi. Things that are now so good in the UK such as farmers' markets and coffee shops were thriving in Sydney a decade and a half ago. I used to love walking through the Victorian suburb of Paddington, with its eye-candy coffee shops, and into Darlinghurst, referred to as 'Darling it hurts' by a local gallery owner I met! Pyrmont Fish Market on a Saturday morning was a favourite weekend destination; the huge tunas always captivated me. It's the second-biggest fish market in the world after Tsukiji in Tokyo.

When I fluff up milk for my coffee at home I always remember my training at Bar Contessa, in the beautiful Balmain district of Sydney. To get the most solid bubble structure it is best to use milk cold from the fridge; once heated, leave it to stand for a few minutes before pouring into the coffee cup. That was the easy part. I then had to decide whether or not I should charge the older Italian and Greek men taking a late morning espresso – they were possibly acquaintances or extended family of the owners, and I did not want to embarrass either them or myself by asking an honorary patron for cash.

Biscotti for coffee

110g almonds
135g caster sugar
2 eggs
1 teaspoon vanilla extract
225g plain flour
1 teaspoon baking powder
pinch of salt
110g dark chocolate, chopped
    into chunky pieces

makes 16–18 biscotti

Most European countries have adopted their own version of biscotti: the English have rusks; the French, *biscotte* and *croquets de Carcassonne*; the Germans, *zwiebacke*; the Greeks, *biskota* and *paxemadia*; the Jews, *mandelbrot*; and the Russians, *sukhariki*.

It is very satisfying to have a clear glass jar filled with biscotti on hand over the Christmas holiday period. A good friend of mine accidentally ordered 14 packets of biscuits online with her trigger-happy mouse, but said that she felt prepared for anything, knowing that her cupboard was stockpiled with jammie dodgers!

Preheat the oven to 180°C/gas mark 4. Toast the almonds for 8–10 minutes on a baking sheet, until they are light brown. When cool, chop them up.

Beat the sugar, eggs and vanilla extract together in a mixing bowl until the mixture is pale and fluffy. In a separate bowl, sift the flour with the baking powder and salt, then add this to the egg mixture. Beat together until it is all mixed, then fold in the almonds and chocolate pieces.

Roll the dough into a log that's about 30cm long and bake on a baking tray for about 25 minutes, until it is firm to the touch. Cool on a rack for about 10 minutes. Turn the oven down to 160°C/gas mark 3.

Cut the log into diagonal slices to form the biscotti, place on a baking sheet and cook for 10 minutes a side.

Orange, chocolate and ricotta muffins

wet ingredients
320ml milk
250g ricotta cheese
2 eggs
1 tablespoon orange flower
    water
60g butter, melted

dry ingredients
325g plain flour
200g sugar
2 teaspoons baking powder
½ teaspoon salt
grated zest of 1 orange
150g dark chocolate, chopped
    into large chunks

makes 14–16

These are the antitheses of the dry, crumbly, cellophane-wrapped muffins of the packaged variety, as the ricotta gives them a springy texture and intimate moistness. Breaking one open reveals a chocolate and orange-flecked interior. This trio of flavours work together brilliantly in pretty much any incarnation, whether it be a cheesecake, tart, cake or ice cream.

I love baking the muffins in these rustic-looking paper cases. After some elementary-level origami with the parchment paper, however, like most 'simple' looking things, they require a fair bit of construction time. On a more functional level the muffins do peel away better from these lovingly hand-crafted paper cases, and you get the added benefit, as my lovely sociology teacher would have said, of being fully involved in the whole creative process – create muffin case, make muffins, eat muffins, wash muffin tray, recycle muffin cases… These are great for taking on picnics, as they stay whole in the lugging-food-to-the-destination process.

Preheat the oven to 180°C/gas mark 4. Measure out the milk in a measuring jug, add the other wet ingredients, and beat gently. Put the dry ingredients into a large mixing bowl and stir through.

Add the wet ingredients to the dry ones and stir, but not too enthusiastically – the mixture doesn't need to be super smooth. Spoon into standard-sized muffin cases – or home-made ones – placed in a muffin tin and bake for 20–25 minutes. Let them cool in their tray for 5 minutes, then cool on a wire rack.

Bar Contessa was an Italian coffee shop run by two couples, one Greek and the other Italian. The parents of one of the Italian owners had run the only Italian restaurant in Alice Springs. Just before I left they bought a great white convertible Rolls Royce in which we used to tour rival coffee shops in the area. The café was a successful combination of urban sleek and the home comfort of hand-made bakery products seductively on view on glass-domed pedestals and woven baskets. There were muffins for all: pneumatic blueberry ones, mostly bought for children and their grannies; apple and bran ones for the healthy set and the models chatting to their agents; and carrot and walnut – I think

the staff polished these off. Terraced between two other shops, it had a floor-to-ceiling wall of glass, enabling us to be voyeurs of the outside world, while passers by could watch café life taking its course on the other side of the pane. At eight o'clock in the morning when we opened up we would turn up the Van Morrison and I would start slicing the focaccia mountain for the lunch brigade, with an extra-long, serrated knife. Just reeling off the menu names – Rockmelon Smoothie, Zucchini and Eggplant Focaccia, Mini-mozzarella Bocconchini, Bacci Chocolate Kisses on the counter – puts me back on the shop floor.

Zesty pistachio and polenta cake

250g butter, softened
250g caster sugar
3 eggs
100g polenta
250g ground almonds
1 teaspoon baking powder
juice and grated zest of 1 lemon

for the syrup
1 tablespoon caster sugar
1 teaspoon ground cardamom
juice of 1 lemon

75g pistachios, chopped

makes 8–10 slices.

When I first made this cake I was so excited: I had arrived at platform cake nirvana. I couldn't stop taking pictures of it: as I walked across the kitchen to clean down a surface, or top up my cup of tea, out of the corner of my eye I would catch another gorgeous glimpse of the cake, with its smouldering looks, that needed to be captured on my memory card.

The addition of a fragrant sugar syrup infused with cardamom subtly alludes to the Spice Trail. Poured over and lovingly massaged into the cake after cooking, it is reminiscent of the syrup that oozes forth from fresh baklava all over the Middle East. If I owned a snazzy seaside café, the kind you find in the cool 'burbs of Sydney, the Atlantic coast of France and now on the south coast of Britain, I would make this cake and have fun guessing who would order it: Nichole Farhi-clad women and men… Boden-clad children…

Preheat the oven to 160°C/gas mark 3. Line a 23cm springform cake tin with baking parchment.

Cream together the softened butter and sugar in a free-standing mixer, or by hand in a large bowl. Add the eggs, one by one, beating well between each addition. Fold in the polenta, ground almonds, baking powder and lemon zest and juice.

Bake in the oven for 45–50 minutes, until the top of the cake has coloured and the centre is firm. Leave the cake in the tin for 10 minutes before placing on a wire rack to cool. When cool, transfer to a serving plate.

Make the syrup by warming the caster sugar with the ground cardamom and lemon juice. Using a thin skewer or a piece of dry spaghetti, punch holes into the surface of the cake. This culinary acupuncture creates a network of sweet stigmata into which you can then drizzle the syrup. I use a small tea strainer for this task, to diffuse the syrup as evenly as I can. Sprinkle with the chopped pistachios. Bliss…

Peach melba ricotta hotcakes

for the hotcakes
250g ricotta
170ml milk
4 eggs, separated
150g plain flour
1 teaspoon baking powder
pinch of salt
50g butter

for the peach melba sauce
50g butter
1 tablespoon caster sugar
1 peach, sliced into 1cm-thick
  slices
100g raspberries

makes 10 medium-sized hotcakes

The year I lived in Sydney, Bill Granger started up his first café – bills – in Darlinghurst. I remember very clearly reading rave reviews, probably by Terry Durack, in the Sydney Morning Herald. Unfortunately, I never did make it there, one of life's regrets, but every friend and family member visiting Sydney has always been waved goodbye with the same request: 'please visit bills for me'. My globe-trotting sister-in-law even came home with a bills music CD, full of laid-back vibe music, an audio wallpaper to a Sunday-morning brunch.

These ricotta hotcakes, the Australian equivalent of American thick pancakes and maple syrup, are light with an underlying touch of creaminess, and are served with lashings of fresh fruit. They really belong to bill (he's so relaxed, he always goes lower case), but have become part of our family weekend ritual.

For the recipe's photo shoot, I had planned to serve these hotcakes with passion fruit and Greek yogurt, but I couldn't track down any passion fruit in my local shops. Thinking on my feet and looking at what was available – some unripe peaches and dark raspberries – I came up with this tasty ensemble.

First make the peach melba sauce. Melt the butter in a frying pan over a moderate heat. Add the sugar and peach slices and cook for 8–10 minutes until softened and glistening. Remove from the heat.

Whisk the ricotta, milk and egg yolks in a large mixing bowl until they have combined. Sift the flour, baking powder and salt into the ricotta mixture and mix together. In another bowl, whisk the egg whites until stiff, then fold into the main mix. Fry in a pan wiped with butter, 2 at a time. They will take about 2–3 minutes each side over a medium heat.

Serve the hotcakes with a generous spoonful of caramelised peach melba sauce on each, a scattering of fresh raspberries and perhaps some Greek Yogurt Ice Cream (see page 70).

Greek yogurt ice cream

310ml double cream
410ml thick Greek natural
  yogurt
200g icing sugar
1 teaspoon vanilla extract

enough for 4–6

The flavours we loved from our recent Italian trip, a kind of modern-day mini-grand tour, were watermelon, zuppa Inglese (trifle), panna cotta and this ice cream. It was one of the highlights of the trip – along with my children singing *A Spoonful of Sugar* and *Chim chim cher-Ee* in Italian with an elderly couple on the train to Rome.

Don't be prejudiced, as I was for weeks, by the bland appearance of this *gelato bianco*. For most of the trip in the gelateria of Venice, Milan and the rural Marche I resisted the flavour (or, in Italian, *il perfumo*), then decided to give it a whirl in Greve, Chianti. The inherent, almost bacterial tang, coupled with the silken cream, is a magical combination, completely multilayered and subtle, unlike ice cream from the commercial big hitters. Looking down the list of ingredients, the whole is definitely greater than the sum of its parts. This was the flavour I most wanted to replicate when we returned home.

Whisk all of the ingredients together in a large mixing bowl, then pour into an ice-cream maker. Let the machine do the work, then enjoy at the glorious soft stage.

If making without an ice-cream maker, put into a covered container and put in the freezer. Give it a good beating every hour for the first 3 hours, to get rid of the ice crystals that form as the ice cream freezes.

In Sydney we were lucky enough to rent a ground-floor apartment on Campbell Parade right on the ocean-front road opposite the Bondi Iceberg Club. This was *real* shabby chic, before it became glammed up and imaginatively rebranded the Bondi Icebergs! We used to walk our breakfast across the road to the grassy verge overlooking the surf break and sit munching on fresh warm brioche and juice while reading the Sydney Morning Herald. Afterwards we would walk around the coastal footpath to Tamarrama, and perhaps grab a coffee in the beach café, before sprawling on the warm flat rocks above the Mackenzie's Bay.

Around the corner into Lamrock Avenue there was an organic fruit and veg shop selling glorious fat pumpkins and zesty greens from hand-made baskets. Nothing came cling-wrapped with a bar code. This might seem normal now, since most places have farm shops and food markets, but 15 years ago this was something of a special shop, with customers that resembled Ben and Jerry.

Three bean salad

90g French beans
175g borlotti beans, cooked
175g pinto beans, cooked
175g chickpeas, cooked
10–15 tender sprigs of thyme
salt and pepper

for the dressing
1 tablespoon honey
1 tablespoon balsamic vinegar
juice of ½ lemon
salt and pepper

enough for 4 as a side dish

I nearly called this a Four Bean Salad, until I remembered that chickpeas are, of course, as the name implies, peas and not beans. The honey and balsamic dressing is a ballsy kind of number that can cope amply with the bean fight.

Trim the ends off the French beans and blanch in plenty of unsalted water for 5 minutes, then drain in a colander and run under a cold tap. Leave to drain.

Put all the ingredients for the dressing in a clean jam jar, shut and shake to mix.

Mix all the beans lightly together in a large serving bowl. Run your fingers down the woody stem of each thyme sprig to scatter the leaves into the bowl. Season, mix the dressing through and serve.

Lime, basil and mandarin salad

for the salad

4 mandarins, segmented

½ cucumber, sliced into long
   shafts

handful of basil leaves, torn

60g toasted pine nuts

1 tablespoon sesame seeds

for the dressing

1 tablespoon caster sugar

juice of 1 lime

1 tablespoon light soya sauce

salt and pepper

enough for 4 as a side dish

Inspiration for cooking comes from many places, including, as here, from a perfume. I always rather fancied the idea of eating rather than smelling Jo Malone's Lime, Basil and Mandarin Cologne, clearly based on a gorgeous Pacific-Rim food combination, so have reincarnated it here as a salad.

This is stunningly good with a great fat wedge of grilled salmon or maybe an oozing steak topped off by a dollop of warm lentil salad. Dream you are having lunch by the sea – in Sydney – just for a moment.

Combine the sugar, lime juice, soya sauce, salt and pepper in a small lidded jar. Shake to mix.

Scatter the mandarin segments, cucumber shafts, torn basil and pine nuts onto a flat platter. Drizzle on the dressing and sprinkle the sesame seeds generously over. Inhale deeply and dab on your neck and wrists if you must!

Courgette, mint and ricotta frittata

4 large waxy new potatoes, with
their skins on, chopped into
halves or quarters (depending
on size)

4–5 tablespoons olive oil

1 large onion, sliced

.1 clove garlic

500g (about 3 medium)
courgettes, sliced

6 eggs

100g ricotta

2 tablespoons chopped mint

salt and pepper

enough for 5–6

I used to make a seasonal vegetable frittata in my tiny, virtually windowless, kitchen in Bondi to sell on to the customers at Bar Contessa. It varied according to the produce I had and what was in season. One day it might be red pepper and rocket, the next, artichoke and black olive. For my perfect frittata pan I now use a Spanish *cazuela* as it can be placed on direct heat, but also go into the oven. You can tinker with the quantities to suit your own vessel.

I have chosen a courgette frittata recipe. Let's face it, if you grow courgettes (and two plants are definitely enough), you'll need a creative outlet for your produce.

Boil the potato until part-cooked in a pan of salted water – this should take about 7–10 minutes. Drain and set aside.

In a large ovenproof pan, heat the oil over a moderate heat, add the onion and garlic and cook for 5–6 minutes to soften, but not brown. Add the courgette and stir until coated in the garlicky oil. Sauté for 5–7 minutes to soften. Add the potato and stir through. Preheat the oven to 180°C/gas mark 4.

In a jug, whisk together the eggs, ricotta and mint and season well. Pour this over the potato and courgette mixture. Cook for a further 5 minutes, then transfer to the oven until the top is golden and feels springy to the touch.

After a day's work at Bar Contessa I would take the ferry home to Circular Quay and, in the evening, jump over the locked-up gate to the Iceberg Club. With a few others we would swim lengths in the salty sea-water pool hewn into the rocks. It reminded me of swimming in a similar pool in Bude, North Cornwall, during my childhood holidays, and seemed surreal: you could work in one of the biggest cities in the world and yet, in the same city, kick back on a beach and swim. A little bit of holiday, every day.

Roast sausages with sweet potato, aubergine and feta

500g good-quality pork
   sausages
3 large sweet potatoes, sliced
   into carrot-sized shards
10 sprigs of thyme
salt and pepper
4–5 tablespoons olive oil
2 medium aubergines, cut into
   thick pieces
200g feta cheese

enough for 4

It's typical that, as I finish the photography and writing for this book, I cook a meal from veg-box leftovers and some feta found at the back of the fridge, and produce one of the tastiest evening meals we've enjoyed this autumn. This recipe really does require minimum attention. Every now and again you need to toss the lot around, in the portal of the oven, but you can gently maintain the extra-curricula comings and goings of a busy household while this meal makes itself.

Preheat the oven to 200°C/gas mark 6.

In a large roasting tin, arrange the sausages and shards of sweet potato. Sprinkle over the sprigs of thyme and season with salt and pepper. Dredge with a good glug of olive oil and turn the sausages and sweet potatoes to coat.

Cook in the oven for 20 minutes, then remove and stir everything together. Place the aubergine pieces on top, giving them a good

drink – about 3 tablespoons – of olive oil. Return to the oven and cook for a further 25–30 minutes until the sausages are cooked and the sweet potato and aubergine are meltingly tender.

Remove from the oven, crumble the feta directly into the roasting tin, and serve directly. A late-season salad of chicory and rocket, with a spritz of lemon juice and a hit of seasoning, would be a welcome partner with some warm flatbread and yogurt.

One evening as I sat in the Greek Consulate General's house, overlooking the ocean at Cogee Bay in Sydney, I remember thinking: this is a gorgeous meal and great company, a beautiful house in a stunning location. We were eating a feta and ricotta tart, and there was an oily octopus and sharp cucumber salad as well. I've added some thyme to my version of the tart, or you could toss in the small-leafed variety of Greek basil, for a regional resonance.

Feta and ricotta tart with poppy seed pastry

for the pastry

250g shortcrust pastry, made with 180g plain flour and 90g butter (see page 8 for method)

2 tablespoons poppy seeds

1 egg, beaten

for the filling

250g ricotta cheese, at room temperature

200g feta cheese, at room temperature

2 egg whites, lightly beaten

1 heaped teaspoon chopped fresh thyme

serves 4–6

To be honest, the recreation of this tart eluded me for ages. I remembered equal quantities of ricotta and feta, with a few eggs and little else. Then I came across Nigella Lawson's Baked Ricotta with Grilled Radicchio in *Forever Summer* and hit upon the idea of using egg whites to bring the ricotta and feta together. Thank you.

Preheat the oven to 190°C/gas mark 5. Roll out the chilled pastry to fit a 20cm tart tin, sprinkling on the poppy seeds and rolling them in as you go. Bake the pastry blind for about 15 minutes. Prick with a fork, brush with beaten egg, and leave to cool. Turn down the oven to 180°C/gas mark 4.

Stir the ricotta and feta together in a large mixing bowl. Whisk in the beaten egg whites and thyme and season with salt and pepper. Pour into the pastry case and cook in the oven for about 35–40 minutes. Remove from the oven and leave to sit for 5 minutes before removing from the tin. Enjoy warm.

Home at Bigbury on Sea

When I returned from living in Sydney, I think I always, under the surface, wanted to recreate that way of life. I had an urge to live by the coast again. Eventually, we were able to build a new house on the site of a run-down '50s beach-style chalet in Bigbury on Sea. We could now live out our Sydney fantasy – in Devon.

Our beach house overlooks the eccentric Art Deco Burgh Island, with its hotel favoured by Noël Coward and Agatha Christie, and beautiful Bigbury Bay. The whitewashed pub on the island, The Pilchard Inn, is named after the dolphins that come here for the warm water and not, surprisingly, for the cocktails in the hotel bar or the eclectic fish menu. Bigbury Bay oysters, mussels and sea bass are tantalisingly close. Watching the surfers in the river mouth reminds me of similar daily escapes in Sydney and further up the New South Wales coast around Byron Bay. I feel as though I should be on my surf ski, harvesting our supper from the sea before the boys get dropped off in their dinky-size yellow school bus.

In Edwardian times, Bigbury was advertised as a health spa and, during its heyday in the interwar period, had a good number of hotels and wooden self-catering chalets. These have all gone now apart from two: one on the mainland and the other on Burgh Island. The latter can be reached by walking across a sandy causeway at low tide, or alternatively, you can take a sea tractor through the waves once the east and west tides have met.

A small rocky chain, called the Murrays, looks as if it is about to tow the island across the bay. Across the blowy headland opposite our house the rabbits scoot as they hear you coming and the furry ball caterpillars we call 'furry murrys' snuggle up in the dry tusky grass. Secret low-water coves, such as Fairy Cove with its iridescent white pebbles and bird and rabbit skulls bleached by the sun, are possible expeditions nearby.

Small pods of dolphins can sometimes be seen in Bigbury Bay, although the last time I saw them was a few years ago. A friend who lives opposite the beach called up to let me know they were there so I bundled toddler Raz and baby Bear into a double buggy and raced down the hill, pointing them out to an appreciative Raz, while baby Bear slept on.

Quick-fire squid with extra heat

1kg squid, cleaned, scored on
   the inside and cut into strips
2 tablespoons olive oil
2 cloves garlic, crushed
1 long red chilli, seeded and
   finely chopped
juice and grated zest of 1 lemon
1 heaped tablespoon each
   chopped coriander, flat-leaf
   parsley and oregano
salt and pepper

serves 4–6 as part of a larger menu

It's best to go for the small cephalopods here, as they taste tender under quick-fire cooking conditions. I once had some deep-fried squid rings along the New South Wales Coast that were so tender, they had the texture of cod!

This dish is good as part of a larger barbecue menu, and can be extended into a full-blown lunch meal by throwing in some rocket or mizuna leaves and perhaps some slithers of red onion that have been waiting in wine vinegar.

Mix together all the ingredients in a bowl and marinate for 2–3 hours.

Heat a large ridged griddle, barbecue or frying pan over a high heat. Add the squid and cook for 1–2 minutes on each side until just cooked – take care not to overcook as if you do it will be tougher than an elastic band!

Mackerel burgers with caramelised onion relish

for the burgers

4 mackerel fillets, cooked and
     flaked

1 large onion, finely chopped

1 clove garlic, finely chopped

200g breadcrumbs

1 egg, beaten

1 handful of parsley, chopped

for the onion relish

5 medium red onions, finely
     sliced

2 tablespoons olive oil

1 tablespoon Demerara sugar

2 cloves garlic, crushed

1 tablespoon red wine vinegar

salt and pepper

3–4 tablespoons olive oil for
     frying

8 floury white baps

makes 8 burgers

As soon as I realised that I wanted a piscine alternative to the standard burger, I decided that I needed an appropriate fishy vehicle, and an equally unwimpish relish, resonant of the traditional beef burger, to smear in the bap.

You can modify the flavour of the burgers by using different types of mackerel. I have used smoked and honeyed mackerel for these, but straight mackerel or peppered mackerel fillets would all work well. I've kept potato out of the burger, so as not to stray into fishcake territory (although I don't suppose the piscine police would press any charges) and to allow for some large chips, of the hand-cut variety, to cheerfully ride alongside.

In a large mixing bowl, place the flaked mackerel, chopped onion, garlic, breadcrumbs, beaten egg and parsley. Lightly mix with a fork. Make into burger shapes, compressing them on a board, then place in the fridge while you make the onion relish.

In a large frying pan over a low heat, fry the finely sliced onion in the olive oil until it is soft and translucent. Add the sugar, garlic and red wine vinegar. Cook for a further 20 minutes and remove from the heat. Season to taste.

Fry the burgers on both sides for about 7 minutes a side. Serve each burger in a floury bap with the caramelised onion relish, homemade chips and perhaps some good quality mayonnaise, spiked with a little fresh dill.

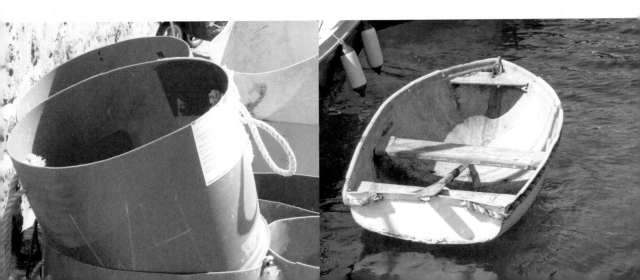

Fish stowaway

approximately 300g fish such as
    salmon, bream, bass or trout
    (whole fish, steak or fillet)
1 clove garlic, peeled and
    squashed with the back
    of a knife
1 slice of lemon
sprigs of fennel fronds, thyme
    and flat-leaf parsley
knob of butter

serves 1

I love the way in which the paper both veils and reveals its fishy passenger inside. It's more than fine to eat the fish straight from its wrapper or put it in some barbecued flatbread with my Roasted Beetroot, Feta Cheese and Clementine Salad (see page 87) and some Greek yogurt.

Season the fish (on the inside, if using whole fish) with the squashed garlic, slice of lemon, a few herb sprigs and a blob of butter. Take a rectangle of greaseproof paper (white is nice) to make a generous envelope around the fish. Put the fish in the centre, pull up the sides and fold over the join a couple of times to seal the parcel.

If cooking in the oven, preheat to 200°C/gas mark 6. Place the fish parcel on a large baking tray and cook for about 15 minutes. Or place the parcel on a barbecue for the same amount of time, until the flesh is opaque all the way through. Eating the fish straight from the parcel is a real 'on the beach' event.

Roasted beetroot, feta cheese and clementine salad

300–350g bunch of beetroot,
    preferably with fresh-looking
    leaves
3–4 tablespoons olive oil
salt
1 tablespoon fennel seeds
2 clementines, peeled and
    segmented
100g beet leaves or a mixture of
    robust salad leaves such as
    rocket, mizuna, etc.
200g feta cheese

for the dressing
1 tablespoon balsamic vinegar
2 tablespoons olive oil
salt and pepper

serves 4

If you have an allotment or your own veggie patch, then beetroot will most likely be a familiar summer friend. Regular eaters will know that it... well… makes you regular, that is, with the benefit of an imperial hue. The pairing of beetroot and fennel seeds is sublime and effortlessly earthy. Fennel grows wild abundantly on the south coast of Devon and is always popping up in unexpected corners of the garden. Scandinavians eat sack loads of it! This is another north-meets-south recipe, with the beetroot's northern aroma mingling with the Mediterranean, if not Middle Eastern, flavour of fennel seed. If you have any of the salad left over it can, without the clementine perhaps, be used as a beautiful, autumnal-looking pizza topping.

Preheat the oven to 200°C/gas mark 6. Lightly scrub the beets and cut into smallish chunks of about 1.5cm. Place in a large roasting tin, drizzle generously with the olive oil, and sprinkle with salt and the fennel seeds. Roast in the oven for 30–40 minutes. Leave to cool.

Whisk the dressing ingredients together in a small jug.

To assemble the salad, scatter the clementine segments, salad leaves, feta and roasted beets in a shallow salad bowl, then drizzle the dressing lightly over the whole salad before serving. I try to avoid tossing this salad as the purple beet juice will run all over the goat's cheese, although it can look good with a bit of 'purple rain', as in the picture opposite.

Naked broad bean salad

250g shelled broad beans

250g mixed salad leaves (purslane and a red-tinged oakleaf work well)

2 spring onions, thinly sliced

1 ripe avocado, sliced

1 tablespoon poppy seeds

1 tablespoon hemp seeds

for the dressing

1 heaped teaspoon finely chopped mint

1 heaped teaspoon finely chopped chives

1 tablespoon white wine vinegar

3–4 tablespoons olive oil

salt and pepper

enough for 4 on the side

This is good for early and mid-season broad beans, which are still sweet and full of texture. From a purely aesthetic point of view, the glaucous poppy seeds give the salad a gorgeous grey-blue accent, as well as some small-time crunch.

Cook the broad beans in a pan of briskly boiling water; they should take about 4–5 minutes. Drain, cool them under cold running water, and then de-case them from their shells with your fingers.

Make the dressing by stirring all the ingredients together in a small jug. Adjust the seasoning to your taste.

Put the salad leaves in a bowl with the sliced spring onions and avocado. Sprinkle over the broad beans and most of the poppy and hemp seeds. Drizzle the dressing over, then add the remaining seeds just before serving.

Sometimes an old surfing friend of ours catches sea bass with a line that trails off his long-board in Bigbury Bay. We've yet to catch anything edible off our canoe – just a lone brown croc, of the shoe variety.

Green bean, dill and warm lemon salad

100g green beans
1 large red onion, sliced
50g butter
1 tablespoon maple syrup
juice of 1 lemon
handful of rocket, chopped
100g toasted pine nuts
2–3 tablespoons chopped dill

enough for 4, with a piece of oily fish from the barbecue

This is full-on flavour and texture and provides a good bed, or a fairly rustic duvet, under which to rest a chunky piece of barbecued oily fish. I like to add the rocket in two hits for a layered effect: an ambient background sludge of partially cooked leaves, then snapping fresh ones to finish off the dish. The salad is good cold or warm, and can cope with a fair amount of jiggling around inside a container, or in the car, on its final journey. Definitely one for the road!

Cook the green beans in boiling water for 2–3 minutes, then drain.

Fry the slices of onion in the butter in a frying pan and add the maple syrup once the onions have softened. Stir in the green beans, lemon juice, half of the rocket, half of the pine nuts, and the dill. Continue cooking for 5 minutes, then remove from the heat and finish by adding the rest of the rocket and pine nuts.

Green sauce

handful of thyme sprigs, leaves
   picked off
handful of oregano, finely
   chopped
handful of chives, finely
   chopped or snipped
2 cloves garlic, crushed
3 tablespoons olive oil
pinch of sea salt
pinch of pepper

makes about a cupful

By any stretch of the imagination this is not an authentic salsa verde, which hails from Lombardy in the north of Italy, is big on parsley and omits garlic. But this is the most useful summer sauce, a kind of summer antithesis to the usual ketchup-and-carb pairing. It's great on warm new potatoes, any salad, in an omelette or a soufflé, or drizzled over barbecued meat, fish or halloumi-and-vegetable kebabs.

Finely chop all the herbs and mix in a mortar with a pestle, along with the garlic, olive oil and salt and pepper. This sauce will keep for up to a week in an airtight jar in the fridge. With a bit of lateral thinking you'll end up pulling it out of the fridge to drizzle on pizzas, cheese on toast, salads and more.

Rocket and feta tart

250g shortcrust pastry, made
  using 180g plain flour and
  90g cold butter (see page 8
  for method)
200g rocket
200g feta cheese
6 eggs, lightly beaten
salt and pepper

enough for 4–6

Little salty cubes of feta in a tangled web of rocket, being given its own tart? Fabulous. It is strident and salty and deserves a soft-leafed salad, such as one of the Butterhead type. The rocket could be substituted with equal quantities of sorrel or watercress.

Preheat the oven to 190°C/gas mark 5. Roll out the pastry and use it to line a 30cm tart tin. Bake blind for 15–20 minutes, then remove the tart case and turn down the oven to 180°C/gas mark 4.

Crumble the feta into the tart case and add the torn rocket. Pour over the egg mixture and season. Bake in the oven for 30–35 minutes, until it feels springy in the middle. Leave to sit in the tart tin for 5 minutes before slicing and serving.

Apple galette

500g puff pastry
6 apples, peeled, cored and
    sliced into thin segments
50g caster sugar
50g butter
juice of 1 lemon
3 tablespoons apricot jam
50g pistachios

makes 10–12 slices

This tray-sized tart with fanned, sliced apples is perfect for large-scale gatherings; think barbecue, child's birthday. It can be scaled up very easily, or you can make two of these in tandem without much extra effort. It can also be prepared ahead of time and served cold with cream. Children enjoy 'painting' the tart with apricot jam and sprinkling on the pistachios. I used organic golden delicious the last time I made this and they didn't oxidize while I cut and arranged them, and they tasted fab too! I tend to cut the galette into postcard-sized pieces and encourage guests to eat it like pizza.

Preheat the oven to 190°C/gas mark 5.

On a counter top dusted with flour, roll out the puff pastry into a rectangle to fit a large baking sheet. Score a rim an inch or so from the edges.

Lay the sliced apples across the pastry in rows of opposing directions (see picture opposite), leaving the scored rim clear. Scatter the sugar over the whole tart, dot with blobs of butter and squeeze half the lemon juice over.

Cook for 15–20 minutes, until the apples are cooked through (test with a knife) and the pastry is golden. Set aside to cool.

In a small pan, heat the jam and remaining lemon juice until runny. Then, with a pastry brush, paint the cooled tart all over, including the pastry edge, and sprinkle with pistachios, like glitter on a home-made Christmas card.

Deep chocolate sorbet

165g caster sugar

75g cocoa

450ml water

150g dark chocolate, broken
  into pieces

serves 4–5

You'll find chocolate sorbet in all the *gelateria* in the back streets of Rome, but it is quite an unusual flavour in Britain, which is more into its fruit sorbets. A buttery biscuit, like shortbread, goes well with this luxurious sorbet. Get an ice-cream maker, the kind with a bowl that sits in your freezer. They cost less than the price of a new toaster.

Put the sugar, cocoa and water into a pan and bring to the boil. Add the dark chocolate pieces and stir until they have melted. Leave to cool. Once completely cold, put into an ice-cream maker and churn according to the manufacturer's instructions.

If making by hand, transfer the cooled mixture to an airtight container and put in the freezer. Take out of the freezer once an hour for the first 3 hours when semi-frozen, to give it a good stir, then leave it in the freezer until completely frozen. Take the sorbet out of the freezer 15 minutes before eating.

The working part of the day shrivels into insignificance when the children are home from school and we have supper on the beach. This might be a hasty barbecue tossed into a backpack or bowls of pasta carbonara cooked at home, then rucksacked down to the beach and devoured by the rock pools. Food for the beach needs to be highly charged, flavour packed and squeaky fresh. My brother recently reminded me of an '80s food campaign by a high street frozen-food giant. The laughable tagline was 'if you want it fresh, buy it frozen'! Hilarious food marketing at it's '80s worst, and no more relevant today than it was 20 years ago.

It's always such a treat to go over to Burgh Island in the evening for supper at the Art Deco hotel. You take the sea tractor, and if it's dark, with the tide in full swing and a swell running, the inky black water is almost up to the level of your feet on the tractor platform. The headlights catch the white horses as they meet their match from the other side of the bay. It feels like a real adventure, condensed into a five-minute journey, out across the water wearing your finest. It's all '30s glam inside: parquet floors, curvaceous architecture and a cocktail bar with a gloriously camp fountain and pool. The real, almost natural pool, the Mermaid's Pool, is outside beneath the hotel. It is a sea pool that has been captured by a wall on the lower side to make a beautiful semi-wild swim. At night you can see it illuminated under a green-tinged light.

When we last visited the hotel we were loaned bow ties by Gary the cocktail bar manager to wear into the dining room. Apparently, Melvin Bragg had been dining there the week before us; he had to wear a bow tie, and so did we.

During the week I get my food from a variety of places: my local food stores, farm shops, the once-a-month farmer's market in Kingsbridge, a weekly organic fruit and veg box and fortnightly meat box left on the doorstep, and the beginnings of some home-grown produce from my strip on the allotment.

I even admit to the occasional trip to the supermarket. Different approaches suit different situations. Because of where I live, and my desire not to get into the car every day, I have a large fridge and freezer and stock up when I'm out and about. I always try and group my jobs together, so if I find myself in the local town collecting my son from his drama club, then I'll pop into the veg shop and the butchers opposite. We are certainly off the radar here for any kind of take-away unless, I have been told, we drive to the other end of the tidal road and *rendezvous* at the bottle bank with the local pizza take-away motorcycle from Kingsbridge!

I am conscious that, for our weekday suppers, as a family we tend to have a rotating line-up of risottos, fishcakes, pasta-based dishes and local pork and apple sausages with mash and onion gravy. I sometimes feel guilty that we haven't had much fish on the menu *chez nous* recently and need a break from meat to make way for some superfood-packed vegetarian dishes.

Mid-week morsels
after school, after work, after the weekend has finished...

It is a common feeling that few of us live up to today's domestic ideal, whether that be Victorian Mrs Beeton or contemporary Nigella Lawson. The aspiring middle classes during Mrs Beeton's era, a short one considering she died when she was just 28 after a mere 18 months of domestic experience under her belt, would have found it frustratingly difficult for their industrialised lives to mirror the kind of pastoral idyll that features in her *Book of Household Management*. Mrs Beeton's call to use fresh milk directly from the udder in certain recipes must have left urban Victorian women feeling collectively inadequate as they poured their souring city milk.

I hope that I am not accused in a similar vein. Please don't email me complaining that one of my recipes demanded the scallops should be gathered naked at dawn, on a neap tide, with a bucket made from the last-to-be-mined Cornish tin. Obviously, I can do such things from my coastal hot spot, but I wouldn't want you to feel inadequate!

Although I do love cooking off piste – deciding what to cook at about 6.30pm, depending on the contents of my fridge – I find weekday suppers less of a scary culinary void, and the children get fed at a more socially respectable time, if I do some forward planning and factor in some meals that can be cooked in advance. I love Isabella Beeton's example of this: 'for turtle soup... cut off the head of the turtle the preceding day'! I can't quite compare in the same breath lazily knocking up a four-hour beef stew that virtually cooks itself in the oven while the children are at school with dramatically despatching a turtle for tomorrow's broth. But it's part of the same no-nonsense approach to everyday cooking that has been carried down from generation to generation and is still practised today.

Weekday suppers for me either have to be full-on fresh produce that doesn't need much fussing around with, such as a plain grilled steak with Lime, Basil and Mandarin Salad (see page 74), or meals that take a tiny amount of time to prepare but have long, slow cooking such as Salmon and Marrow Casserole (see page 136). Most importantly, all my food can be made alongside the rest of life, replying to emails, stacking the dishwasher or knocking back some vino.

My early morning weekday fantasy would be to wake at 7am and go for a swim in the sea or pool, then return for a breakfast of freshly squeezed juice, home-made granola, yogurt and berries and a sublime coffee. A copy of the paper wouldn't go amiss either. However, the pre-school morning dash tends to interrupt this ideal and we have weekday breakfast phases: porridge with blueberries, granola with thick Greek yogurt and a drizzle of honey, sometimes pancakes, but more often cereals. It's undeniably hectic making sure three children are fed, dressed, have all their kit ready and are on the bus by 8.20am. The mad sprint down the steps to the often waiting bus is better than a double espresso as an effective shot of wake-up potion.

A jarful of granola helps...

dry ingredients
500g rolled oats
200g buckwheat flakes
50g pecans, in large pieces
50g almonds, halved
200g sunflower seeds
100g linseeds
100g sesame seeds

wet ingredients
1 tablespoon pure cane
   molasses
3 tablespoons runny honey
3 tablespoons sunflower oil
250ml water

fruit
50g dried cranberries
50g dried apricots
50g dried apple

3 vanilla pods

makes 3 litres

Some of the best granolas available in delis and farm shops can make fresh truffles seem like an affordable option. It's always interesting how 'poor man's' grains such as oats, buckwheat and polenta can, with some minor tinkering, become the food of the never-too-rich-nor-too-thin.

I was interested to find out that granola, as a product, dates back at least a century, when it was invented for Victorian spa-goers in Dansville, New York, by a Dr Jackson, whose cereal was known as 'Granula'. A similar cereal was developed by the original Mr Kellogg, John Harvey Kellogg, who used the name 'Granola' to avoid legal problems with Jackson.

My revolving loop of breakfasts has definitely got stuck on this one for the moment. A few heaped spoonfuls of granola, thick full-cream Greek yogurt, milk and berries is the way I love to start the day in summer. I then aim for a coastal run, after the children are safely on their way to school.

This granola was something I used to make as a teenager at home (along with peppermint creams and pasta with pesto), having loved the first commercially produced 'crunchy muesli'. Even then, I was amazed how easy and satisfying the simple mixing and roasting activity was. The recipe has grown over the intervening years to include some over-used superfoods such as cranberries and buckwheat, and some personal favourites such as whole Hunza apricots (don't the people from the Hunza Valley live longer than anyone else on the planet?), pecans and vanilla, the last of which infuses the jar with its sweet creamy aroma.

It's a small investment of time and cash to purchase the grains and nuts initially, but the quantities given below will make enough for a family for a good couple of weeks, and then you'll be able to return to your store cupboard for the next fix.

Preheat the oven to 180°C/gas mark 4.

Mix all the dry ingredients in a large mixing bowl. Cut the fruit into small pieces and set aside.

Whisk together the molasses, honey, oil and water. Add this sticky sweet mixture to the grains, nuts and seeds and mix until everything is moist and starts to clump together a little.

Spread out the mixture over two large baking trays and bake in the oven for about 30 minutes. You need to keep an eye on it during cooking and stir and shake it a few times to achieve an even golden colour and crunchy texture.

Leave to cool, then mix in the fruit. Store in an airtight jar with the vanilla pods thrust into the granola vertically.

Honied figs

5 figs

3–4 tablespoons ricotta cheese

1 tablespoon mixed pumpkin, sesame and sunflower seeds

3 tablespoons runny honey

salt and pepper

enough for 4–5 as a light lunch

Whether they are a soft lichen green, ochre yellow or a musky purple, the beauty of figs lies in their Caravaggio-esque contrast of downy exterior and seductive and sensual, fleshy interior.

This is a great dish in which to try out a single flower honey, as it will allow the individual flavour to shine through. Bear, my middle child, loves to try the different honeys at the French market in Kingsbridge, from the opaque yellow sunflower through the herb and flower varieties of orange and lemon blossom, lavender, thyme and rosemary, to the dark, amber-coloured eucalyptus and chestnut.

A plateful of these would be great as a light lunch with some sparsely dressed salad leaves and bread.

Cut each fig in half, keeping the bases intact, and put them into an ovenproof dish – it should be a snug fit. Spoon one teaspoon of ricotta onto each half, sprinkle with the mixed seeds, laterally drizzle the honey over, and season.

Blast under the grill on its highest setting for about 5 minutes until the seeds have just begun to colour, and the body of the fig has softened and slumped slightly.

Jewelled salad with pomegranate dressing

60g bunch watercress, roughly
   chopped
60g bunch coriander, roughly
   chopped
½ cucumber, chopped into
   small batons
seeds of 1 pomegranate

for the dressing
1 tablespoon pomegranate
   molasses
2 tablespoons olive oil
juice of ½ lemon
salt and pepper

enough for 4 as a side dish

Consider this, along with Honied Figs (see page 106), some fresh
flatbread and some paprika-spiked Greek yogurt, for lunch
with the girls.

Deseed the pomegranate. Then tumble all the salad ingredients
into the serving bowl together and add the pomegranate seeds on
top. Whisk all of the dressing ingredients together in a small jug,
or shake in a lidded jam jar. Dress the salad and toss lightly.

Pappardelle summer salad

250g fresh pappardelle

150g chargrilled artichokes
in oil

100g goat's cheese

25g butter

80g (drained weight) tuna fillets,
such as Ventresca fillets from
Albacore tuna, flaked

50g pea shoots

1 tablespoon olive oil

salt and pepper

1 heaped teaspoon chopped
chives

*enough for 4 as a light bite,
or 2 as the main attraction*

This is exactly the kind of summer lunch I'd like to have mid-week, and I *can* so easily and frequently as I tend to keep all the key ingredients in my store cupboard and fridge on a permanent basis, and use whatever shoots are around.

Cook the fresh pasta (that's one of my post-toddler luxuries) in plenty of salted boiling water for about 2 minutes. Meanwhile, slice the artichokes and goat's cheese into robust slices.

When the pasta is cooked, drain it, put it back in the hot pan, then stir in a blob of butter to prevent it sticking together. Toss the artichokes and cheese into the hot pasta. Add the tuna and pea shoots and give it a stir. A glug of olive oil, some generous seasoning and a few snips of chives complete the dish.

We had what might seem like a bit of a busman's holiday this year, by the sea in Cornwall. Admittedly it's not far from home and shares most of the same language, but the deep west of Penwith, around Zennor and St Ives, feels spectacularly like Brittany and the northwest coast of France, with its granite-lintled buildings, prolific hydrangeas and trifid-like echiums spiralling skywards with their violent finials.
We made a pact to return for a surfing and foodie weekend soon, particularly as we didn't get a chance to visit one of my favourite restaurants, The Porthminster Café on Porthminster beach in St Ives. It was originally an Edwardian white-washed tearoom, situated for day trippers adjacent to the railway station, but is now the most fabulous restaurant; think Serpentine Gallery as a pan-Pacific restaurant on a beach, and you have the idea. When we were last there, sitting in the open doors upstairs, we watched a fisherman with his small boat, more of the Hemmingway variety than the Alfred Wallis, lunge up the pale sand and walk his catch up to the restaurant kitchen. If it wasn't what happens there all the time, I would say that he was a paid 'extra'.

Salmon and lemon thyme fishcakes with brioche crumbs

600g cooked salmon

400g potatoes, cooked and
    mashed without milk
    and butter

3–4 tablespoons chopped lemon
    thyme

grated zest and juice of 1 lemon

salt and pepper

4–5 tablespoons plain flour

1 egg, beaten

200g brioche crumbs

2–3 tablespoons olive oil

makes about 8–10 fishcakes

This is a very British version of a fishcake, with its flesh-coloured salmon interior and floppy-leafed lemon thyme: the Hugh Grant of the fishcake world. It is not so potent as its drier Mediterranean relative, but I love all kinds of fishcake, from the chilli-flecked through to the Scandi-style with lashings of dill.

These fishcakes have a quiet personality. They sit nicely alongside salads, puy lentils or fries when you don't fancy anything dramatic from the kitchen.

Fork together the salmon, mashed potato, lemon thyme, lemon zest and juice and salt and pepper, working gently to produce coarse-textured flakes of salmon. Flour your hands, then shape the mixture into 8–10 cake-shaped rounds that are about 2.5cm thick. Put in the fridge for at least 30 minutes to firm up.

Prepare three bowls – one with the flour, another with the beaten egg and the third with the brioche crumbs. Dip each fishcake first into the flour, then coat with the egg, then finally roll in the brioche crumbs.

Fry in the olive oil over a medium heat on each side for about 5 minutes.

Sweet red onion tart with goat's cheese

250g shortcrust pastry, made
    with 180g plain four and
    90g cold butter (see page 8 for
    method)
2 tablespoons olive oil
5 medium red onions
2 cloves garlic, crushed
1 tablespoon maple syrup
100g goat's cheese, sliced into
    rounds
10–15 sprigs of thyme
salt and pepper

enough for 6, with a feisty salad

This is the perfect midsummer tart, with its claret-red tangle of onions and creamy ingots of goat's cheese. It is a great lunch dish when goat's cheese is at its best from the fresh new-season grass. When we go to the local farmers' market, Beren loves to try the complete selection of goat's cheeses, from the lavender-encrusted to the one with black and pink peppercorn stigmata.

If I can get away without baking the pastry case blind, then I do. The filling isn't runny so it's fine to bake the tart in one hit. The sides flop down and curl over in a soft rustic way – it reminds me of the tarts and pies my grandma used to bake on a Pyrex oven plate.

Roll out the pastry and line a 30cm tart tin with it. Chill the pastry in the fridge while you cook the onion for the filling.

Over a low heat, heat the olive oil a in large, heavy-based frying pan. Add the onion and garlic and stir until the onion is well coated in the oil. Cover the pan with a lid and cook incredibly gently for 20 minutes, then add the maple syrup and cook until the onions are softened, but not coloured; this will be about another 20–30 minutes. Set aside to cool.

Preheat the oven to 190°C/gas mark 5.

Remove the pastry case from the fridge and fill the base with the onion. Dot the goat's cheese around the tart, nestling it in between the onions. Then lay on the sprigs of thyme, sprinkle with a good seasoning of salt and pepper and perhaps splash with a few drops of olive oil. Bake in the oven for 25–30 minutes, until the pastry is cooked.

Pumpkin soup with black olive and feta quesadillas

for the soup

100g butter

2 leeks, chopped

2 cloves garlic, crushed

1.5kg pumpkin or dense squash, such as butternut, chopped into small cubes

1.5l chicken stock

100ml double cream

for the quesadillas

8 tortilla wraps

4 tablespoons black olive tapenade

200g feta cheese

2–3 tablespoons olive oil for frying

enough for 6–8

I love to use a mixture of butternut squash and the beautiful, if sometimes impenetrable, blue-skinned Crown Prince pumpkin. This was my autumn lunch *de jour* in Sydney. I used to devour vast vats of the velvety stuff alongside a toasted focaccia sandwich filled with kalamata olive tapenade. I have upgraded the focaccia sandwich to a slimline quesadilla made from flatbread, such as a tortilla. Along with the black olive and feta filling, this is a much lower carb hit, especially handy if it's going to be lunch.

In a large, heavy-based pan, melt the butter and add the chopped leeks and garlic. Cook over a low to moderate heat until the leeks have softened, but not browned. Add the chopped pumpkin or squash and give it a stir, then add the stock. Let this simmer away with the lid on for about 30 minutes, until the pumpkin is cooked through.

Remove the pan from the heat and allow the mixture to cool slightly. Blitz with a hand-held blender, or decant to a liquidiser and blend to the desired consistency. Stir in the cream, then set to one side.

To make each quesadilla, take a tortilla wrap, spread the tapenade over half of the circle – not going too close to the edge – and scatter with crumbled feta. Fold the sides together and fry on a lightly oiled, ridged griddle or in an oiled frying pan for 2–3 minutes each side, pressing down and flattening the tortilla ever so slightly as it cooks. Slice in two and enjoy with the soup on the side – or is it the other way around?

When the children arrive home from school, during the transition from institution to individual, I might suggest some baking or making. Anything that can be formed into dragons, contains chocolate that needs chopping (one for the mouth, one for the pot) or boasts lurid colours often hits the spot.

We tend to make seasonal batches of playdough; a new one is born as an old either goes hard or gets lost under the sofa. Most parents I know have their own recipe stashed under a magnet on the side of the fridge. Mine contains 200g plain flour, 100g table salt, 2 teaspoons cream of tartar, 1 tablespoon cooking oil, 300ml water and some food colouring. Put everything except the colouring in a large, heavy saucepan on a high heat, stirring constantly for about 5 minutes until the mixture starts to come together. Stir in the food colouring drop by drop and stir for a further 2–3 minutes. Knead the warm dough on a board until the colour is uniform. Store in an airtight container.

Obviously, you probably won't want to eat this, although unlike shop-bought Play-Doh, you can – ingredient for ingredient, it is probably better for you than a standard bag of crisps. Its elasticity comes from the cream of tartar, which is derived from tartaric acid, a by-product of the wine-making process. I usually double or treble the above quantity and split it into separate balls for different colours. It is so much cheaper than buying pots from a shop and for the person doing the making, the kneading and pushing in of the colour into the warm dough is hugely satisfying.

And you get to play with it.

Jam tarts with orange drizzle

for the tarts
250g shortcrust pastry, made using 180g plain flour and 90g cold butter (see page 8 for method)
jam (raspberry, strawberry and blackcurrant all work well)

for the icing
150g icing sugar, sifted
juice of 1 orange

makes about 12

I first made these with leftover shortcrust pastry from a savoury pie adventure, as is the tradition with jam tarts. What follows below is a recipe for making these little beauties from scratch. Modify the icing quantity for the leftover method and spoon from the jam jar as required.

Make the pastry, wrap in clingfilm and put in the fridge to rest for 30 minutes.

Preheat the oven to 200°C/gas mark 6. Roll out the pastry thinly, then cut out rounds with a pastry cutter or glass. Grease a jam tart tin with a piece of butter wrapper. Press the pastry rounds into the holes of the tart tin and fill each one ⅔ full with jam.

Bake for 10–12 minutes, until the pastry is golden and the jam is bubbling excitedly. Cool in the tin for a few minutes before transferring the tarts onto a wire rack.

To make the icing, put the sifted icing sugar in a bowl. Add orange juice, blending it in slowly to make a smooth icing. Drizzle laterally over the cooled tarts.

Local-apple cake

2 eggs
175g caster sugar
1 teaspoon vanilla extract
75ml milk
150g butter, soft
125g plain four
2 teaspoons baking powder
2 local apples

makes about 8 slices

This apple cake is lighter in character than many of the regional cakes from Devon, Somerset and Dorset. All have in common a rich buttery batter, though sometimes raisins are added and some have a sugary topping. There are so many beautiful heritage apples around – in September my local farm shop had Limelight, Katy and my favourites, Russets. The recipe only needs a couple of apples, so try to use ones grown locally.

Preheat the oven to 180°C/gas mark 4.

Line a 20cm x 20cm cake tin with baking parchment. In either a free-standing mixer or a large bowl, beat the eggs, sugar and vanilla together for about 5 minutes. Pour the milk into a small pan to warm and add the butter to melt. Pour the milky, buttery liquid into the bowl with the egg-and-sugar mix, beating all the time. Sift the flour and baking powder together and add to the cake mixture, mixing well to ensure it is lump-free. Pour the batter into the lined cake tin, then peel and slice the apples and arrange on top of the batter mix.

Bake for 25–30 minutes. The cake should have a golden colour and be firm, but give slightly when pressed in the middle.

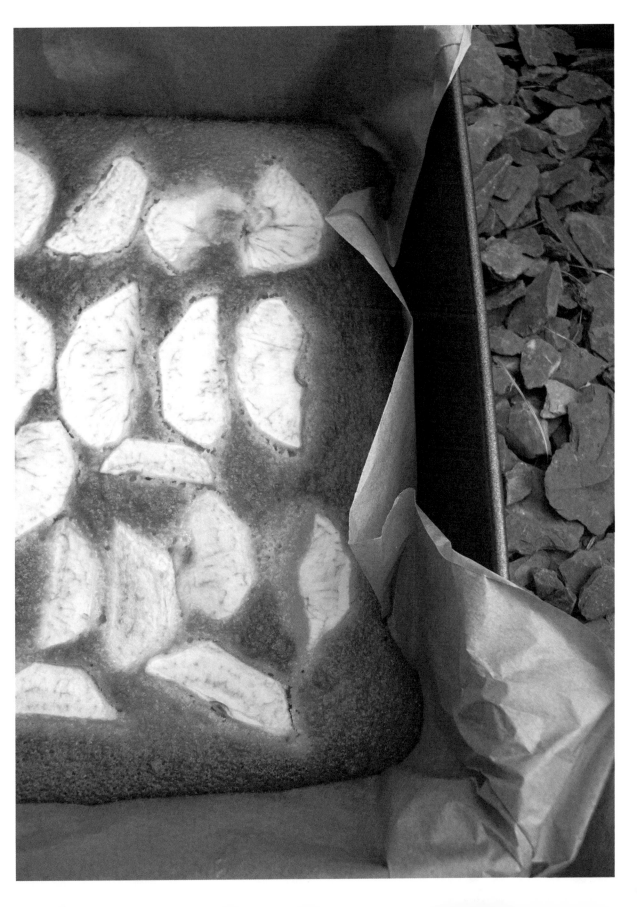

Fairy cakes and muffins always used to be called buns in our house, and I'm beginning to wish that I still had a lack of self-consciousness in these matters and didn't hand-pick labels in my mind, constantly subdividing and re-labelling individual cakes into cupcakes, muffins, bundts and so on. The world was a simpler one, certainly for me at least, when there were only buns. But here we are, in the post-bun age.

Vanilla cupcakes

250g butter
250g sugar
4 eggs
1 teaspoon vanilla extract
200g plain flour
50g self-raising flour
185ml milk
225g golden icing sugar, sieved
2–3 teaspoons hot water
sprinkles

makes about 18 cupcakes

I love the palette of wet-sand colours that golden icing sugar creates. Even my children who, given the choice, would go for pink and blue every time, really appreciate these Farrow & Ball colours – probably called something like Elephant's Breath – that crown each vanilla-laden cakelet.

These are great with friends after dinner, as a post-school tea with the kids or greedily gobbled mid-morning whilst on the phone discussing something *terribly* important.

Preheat the oven to 180°C/gas mark 4. Line your cupcake tins with paper cases.

Cream the butter and sugar together in a large mixing bowl. Add the eggs one at a time, mixing well after each addition, then stir in the vanilla extract.

Sift the flours together and fold into the cake mix, then add the milk slowly. Spoon the mixture into paper cases and bake for 15–20 minutes. Remove from the oven and allow to cool on a wire rack.

For the icing, mix the sieved icing sugar and hot water together until the sugar melts: add just enough hot water to achieve the consistency you need – it should be soft and runny.

Smooth the icing onto each cake, decorating with tasteful sprinkles as you go.

My mid-week suppers tend to fall into two camps: those that are quick from the point of taking out the chopping board to eating from the plate, such as Dreamy Prawn Gnocchi (see page 132), and those that take their time to cook, but demand little in the way of preparation, such as Chicken with Za'tar ad Lemon (see page 139), so household chores and also pleasures can happen in parallel. My 'two-camps' idea isn't, unfortunately, watertight, and the first recipe I present straddles both concepts and contains both a long waiting period – the dough – and a rapid cooking of the pizza!

Free-form pizzas

for the pizza dough
500g strong white bread flour
7g-sachet dried yeast (about
    2 teaspoons)
10g salt
325ml warm water
1 tablespoon olive oil
handful of polenta for dusting

makes 4–5 plate-sized pizzas

toppings
artichoke hearts
egg
goat's cheese rounds
kiln-roast salmon
passata
prosciutto and rocket
roasted beetroot with fennel
    seeds
tuna

oils and savoury sprinkles
olive oil with fresh chilli, lemon
    zest, garlic, salt and pepper
beetroot leaves
chilli flakes
fresh herbs
green sauce (see page 92)
herb salt (see page 186)

My children love to make these in their own shapes – vague dragons, butterflies and so on. A fairly informal shape suits my anti-perfectionist nature, so mine normally end up being organically oval. I get out an array of small bowls and fill them with toppings so that everyone can have a bespoke pizza. I like a thin scrapping of tomato passata on my pizza, but also sometimes go for more of a pizza bianco, with just a thin drizzle of olive oil and some roasted veg. The pizza in the picture is crowned with my favourite topping this summer: fennel-roasted beetroot, goat's cheese and chilli herb oil, topped with richly veined beet leaves.

I tend to make double the following quantity of dough – some people like two, but also, any spare dough can be made into dinky breakfast rolls. There's always someone who wants to pile everything onto the dough – I prefer to go a bit minimalist and pick a veg, a protein, herbs and oil, and decorate scantily.

Mix the flour, yeast, salt and water to form a dough, then mix in the olive oil. Knead the dough for about 10 minutes, until smooth. Place the dough in a bowl, cover with clingfilm or a clean tea towel and leave in a warm place until doubled in size.

Preheat the oven as high as it will go (in Naples, they are all set at about 250°C/gas mark 9+). Divide the dough into 4–5 apple-sized balls and roll out each one to about 5mm thick. Give everyone their own pizza bases and a range of toppings and sprinkles to form their own bespoke pizzas. Place them on a couple of polenta-dusted baking sheets and cook for about 7 minutes.

Pancetta, broad bean and lentil pasta

1 medium red onion, chopped
1 tablespoon olive oil
250g pancetta, chopped
150g puy lentils
1l chicken stock
250g broad beans
250g dried orecchiette pasta

*serves 4–5 with the potential for
leftovers*

I've used the Disney-esque orecchiette ('little ears') pasta for
this, as their shape literally captures the broad beans that fall
into their concave grasp. This is a lovely dish for early summer,
when the broad beans are small and full of sugar and you can
leave their skins on. The lentils add a welcome earthy element.
If you choose to have the leftovers for lunch the following day,
as I did recently when I took a kilner jar full to my printing
workshop, the flavours meld together beautifully overnight in the
fridge, so the increase in depth of flavour will be pronounced.

In a large, heavy pan, cook the onion in olive oil over a medium
heat. After about 5 minutes, when the onion has softened, add
the pancetta and cook for another 5 minutes, until there are
some tasty scrapings on the base of the pan. Stir in the lentils
and pour in the stock. Bring to the boil and simmer, uncovered,
for 25 minutes. Add the broad beans and pasta and cook until the
pasta is done – the sauce will have thickened by then. This dish
stands alone really well, or could be eaten with a hunk of bread.

Andouille

1kg potatoes, peeled
50g butter
4 hard-boiled eggs, halved
250g bunch of spinach or
    chard, lightly blanched for
    3–5 minutes
150g andouille, French garlic
    sausage or salami, sliced
150g grated Emmental or
    Cheddar cheese

enough for 4–5

Most European countries have their quick supper dishes. I
like this one from the Brittany in northern France, where the
traditional meets a contemporary weekday need. Andouille is
a course-grained sausage made from pork, pepper, onions and
most of the gastrointestinal tract of the pig. The word *andouille*
is a bit of a lightweight insult in French, like our 'silly sausage'.
It's difficult to get hold of the real thing outside France, but most
salami-style sausages work well in this context.

Cook the potatoes and mash with the butter. Preheat the oven to
180°C/gas mark 4. Place the mashed potato in a shallow ovenproof
dish that is roughly 25cm x 20cm. Push the boiled eggs and
spinach into the potato. Arrange the slices of andouille across the
top of the potato and top with the grated cheese. Cook in the oven
for 15–20 minutes. If you have made this in advance and need
to reheat from cold, cover the top with foil for 15 minutes, then
remove for the last 5 minutes to give the cheese some colour.

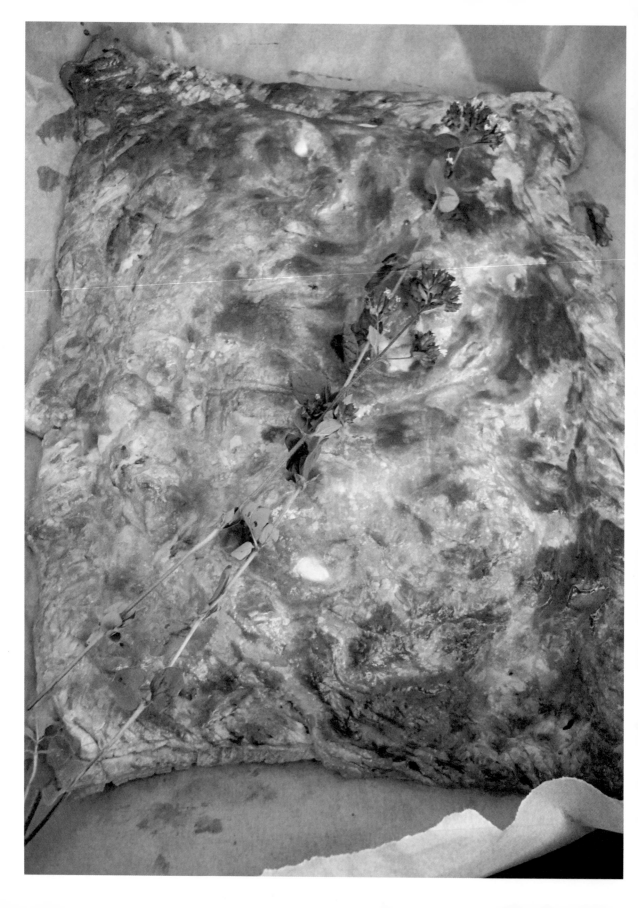

A reassuringly familiar chicken and leek pie

2 leeks, finely sliced

50g butter

2 cloves garlic, crushed

500g chicken (use a mixture of breast and thigh meat), chopped into 2.5cm pieces

100ml double cream

salt and pepper

500g puff pastry

1 egg, beaten

serves 6 generously

This 'pie' is more like a child's pastry envelope, stuffed with nostalgia. I'm not actually sure that I had this a great deal as a child, but cream-laced chicken sauce with translucent strips of melting leek does seem to be part of what psychologists call my autobiographical memory. Making, smelling and eating it all contribute to my feeling a sense of place – and that place is home. There is something about sharing a pie, cutting it – the traditional religious breaking-of-bread analogy – that can make a family or friends come together as one. I seem to make this pie at the end of a stressful week at work, or after an active day at the weekend, walking up the estuary to collect driftwood for kindling.

Along similar stress-induced lines, this would be perfect for Christmas Eve, with the first of the purple sprouting broccoli boiled briskly for 4–5 minutes and seasoned with a hint of lemon juice, sea salt and pepper.

In a heavy pan, melt the butter over a low to moderate heat. Add the leek and garlic and cook for about 8 minutes until soft and translucent. Add the chicken pieces and cook through for about 10 minutes. Pour in the cream, season and stir for another couple of minutes, then remove from the heat to cool.

When the mixture has cooled completely, preheat the oven to 180°C/gas mark 4. Roll out the pastry into a large rectangle and put the chicken mixture on one side of the rectangle to fill just less than half of it, leaving space around the edges for sealing the pastry. Brush around the edges of the pastry with the beaten egg, then fold the pastry over to meet. Press to make a seal, using a fork. Brush the top of the pie with the rest of the beaten egg and bake in the oven for 30–35 minutes.

Dreamy prawn gnocchi

500g vacuum-packed gnocchi
1–2 tablespoons olive oil
250g prawns, cooked
1 red pepper, finely sliced
2 shallots, finely chopped
100ml double cream
2 tablespoon mixed seeds
   (pumpkin, sesame and
   sunflower seeds), plus
   1 tablespoon extra to finish
large handful of baby spinach
   leaves
large handful of basil leaves

*enough for 4, with something on
the side*

This dish reminds me of a time, pre *Ready Steady Cook*, when Diggory and I would spontaneously pop round to a friend's house on a Friday evening after work and construct a main course and dessert from our combined larders.

The combination of gnocchi and cream is truly soporific, and when introduced to strips of red pepper in the pan, turns a fleshy colour, akin to that of apricot fromage frais. I tend to keep prawns and gnocchi in the freezer, so that the exact tone of the finished dish changes more according to the kinds of leaves I add from the fridge or garden. Any salad leaf would suffice – baby gem, radicchio – even though I have used baby spinach and basil here. The only possible exception would be Iceberg lettuce, whose main *raison d'être*, during its brief life, is to be crunchy.

You might think that the only Italian thing about this dish is the tri-colour of pepper, spinach and gnocchi, but the Venetians really go for *gnocchi con scampi*.

First make the sauce by frying the shallots in 1 tablespoon of olive oil over a low to moderate heat. Add in the red pepper slithers after 3–4 minutes and stir around until the peppers slightly soften. Add the cream and, after this has warmed through, add the prawns, seeds, spinach and basil, then take off the heat.

Boil the gnocchi in plenty of salted boiling water for 2–3 minutes, until they bob to the surface. Drain quickly, leaving a little water clinging to the gnocchi (to loosen the waiting sauce), then add them to the pan with the cream sauce. Stir gently over a low heat for 2 minutes.

It's nice to have a fresh layer of seeds scattered over the gnocchi and perhaps a drizzle of olive oil that will slide off the silky potato pillows and puddle enticingly at the bottom.

Italian wedding soup

750g meatballs

2–3 tablespoons olive oil
  or 30g butter

1 large onion, finely chopped

2 stalks celery, finely chopped

3 carrots, finely chopped

1 clove garlic, crushed

500ml water

500ml chicken stock

200g cavolo nero or chard,
  sliced

200g fresh egg spaghetti

handful of flat-leafed parsley,
  chopped

grated parmesan

enough for 6

The idea of having a hearty meatball and pasta soup on the wedding menu really appeals – think *Godfather*-chic. My favourite wedding to date, though, was in France, and it involved an onion soup with brioche at 2am. Having looked into the history of this dish, I have discovered that, in its original form, it was known as 'minestra maritata' or 'married soup'. The marriage refers to the vegetables and meat going well together; in southern Italy, around Naples, they would be known as being 'maritata'. The Italians also use an egg-drop technique, as in Chinese Egg Drop Soup, whereas I prefer to use a fresh egg pasta.

You could use my recipe for Porchetta Meatballs (see page 172) if you fancy making the meatballs from scratch, but omit the fennel seeds and final dusting of polenta (although personally, I welcome fennel at every opportunity).

Cook the meatballs in olive oil or butter in a large pan set over a moderate heat. It should take 7–10 minutes for them to brown off. Put to one side while you make the soup.

Fry the onion in the same pan (you might need to add another splash of oil or blob of butter). When it has softened, add the celery, carrots and garlic. Stir and allow to cook for 5 minutes or so. Add the meatballs, water and stock and simmer for about 15–20 minutes. Put the cavolo nero into the pan with the spaghetti and cook for a further 2–3 minutes. Scatter with some chopped flat-leafed parsley and serve with parmesan.

Salmon and marrow casserole

5–6 salmon steaks
1kg marrow
salt and pepper
handful of thyme (about
    10–15 tender sprigs)
3–4 tablespoons olive oil

serves 5–6

This recipe comes from a friend, Valerie Le Carre, who lives in Brittany. The first time she cooked it was for one of those languorous mid-week working lunches that the French do so well, whereas back home, and left to my own devices, I end up with a ham sandwich.

It is one of those dishes that makes it seem as if you have gone to a great effort. In fact, like most casseroles, you just fling everything in the pan, leave (to go out, go shopping, collect the kids from school), then retrieve from the oven, and eat. What really got me, the first time I had it, was trying to guess what kind of stock Valerie had cooked it in. In fact there is no stock. Merely olive oil, salt and pepper and some herbs. It is the full hour of cooking that gives the marrow in particular its full-bodied, cooked-in stock (but not) flavour. I put this on when I get home from the afternoon school run, and maybe do some creamy mash to go on the side.

Unlike Nigel Slater who, I heard, uses his fish kettle for displaying hyacinths, I feel a genuine desire to put my own kettle (a lovely Christmas present from my mother-in-law) into service when I make this casserole.

Preheat the oven to 180°C/gas mark 4.

Peel and cut the marrow into chunky 2.5cm square cubes and place in the bottom of a large fish kettle or ovenproof casserole. Lay the salmon steaks on top. Season liberally with salt, pepper and thyme and glug over about 3–4 tablespoons of good olive oil.

Cook in the oven for 1 hour. Leave it alone during this time, help the children with their homework, read the paper, take the dog for a walk...

This is great served with some hand-cut chips, roast potatoes or creamy mash.

One of Magi's friend's, a lovely little blonde five-year-old, watched her fluffy chicks grow into adults under the apple trees in her orchard. A beautiful moment, and you would think that the idea of their demise for the pot might come as a shock, but when the day came, she matter-of-factly stated that Goldy was a bit of a bully and would probably taste good.

Chicken with za'tar and lemon

500g chicken wings or thighs
2 cloves garlic, crushed
3 tablespoons olive oil
1 tablespoon za'tar
1 lemon, thinly sliced
200ml water
10 sprigs of thyme

enough for 4–5

My eldest son, Raz, often remarks on the gorgeous smells coming from the kitchen as this cooks in the oven. All the children love it and Magi declares it 'better than beans'. Za'tar (see page 186 for suppliers) is a spicy herb mix – an interesting paradox of flavours, with its earthy, herby, mix of sesame seeds, thyme, oregano, marjoram and sumac. It dates back pretty much unaltered to Mediaeval times, and there were even traces of it found in the tomb of Tutankhamun.

Mix all the ingredients together in a large bowl and leave to marinate for 4 hours.

Preheat the oven to 200°C/gas mark 6.

Tip the ingredients into a large roasting tray and cook for about 30–40 minutes. The kitchen will be filled with a savoury fragrance that neighbours will drool over.

This would be ideal served with a sympathetic salad, such as the Jewelled Salad with Pomegranate Dressing (see page 110), and some warm flatbread.

After the autumn watershed of school footie has moved from the grass pitch to the concrete playground, a carb-based meal calls. In the '70s, on a cold Tuesday in the run-up to Christmas, with the working week still stretching ahead, it would have been steak and kidney pie. We're more likely to have toad in the hole.

Deluxe toad in the hole

12 good-quality pork sausages
12 pieces of pancetta or thin
  rashers of bacon
10–15 sprigs of thyme
2 tablespoons sunflower oil

for the batter
2 eggs
600ml milk
225g plain flour, sifted
salt and pepper

serves 4–6

You need fabulous bangers for this, and can ring the changes with plain pork, pork and herb, pork and black pepper or pork and apple. The 'deluxe' part of the title is the sleeping-bag of bacon wrapped around each sausage. I like to have this with something deep and ferrous, like wilted, buttery spinach.

Make the batter in a large bowl by whisking the eggs and milk together, then whisk in the sifted flour. Season well with salt and pepper and leave to stand, preferably in the fridge, for at least 30 minutes.

Preheat the oven to 180°C/gas mark 4.

Pour the oil into the bottom of the roasting tin. Wrap each sausage in a rasher of bacon, like a pig in a porky straight jacket, and place in the tin. Cook for about 10 minutes, until the bacon and the outside of the sausages are starting to brown.

Turn the oven temperature up to 200°C/gas mark 6 and remove the tin from the oven. If the sausages have let out excess water at this stage, drain off before continuing. Pour over the batter and sprinkle on the thyme. Return to the oven for 30–35 minutes until the batter has puffed pneumatically and is golden brown.

Lovely left-overs, from the weekend Sunday roast, can be resurrected for mid-week treats and full-blown, all-encompassing meals. I like to make a deluxe flatbread wrap using the pink beef from the roast, minty yogurt, chilli flecks, saline shards of Maldon salt, an aerial storm of black pepper and torn coriander. I often roast a little too much root veg than could be reasonably consumed, so that a mid-week soup with some chicken stock and decent bread, is an achievable possibility, if not a definite weekly reality. Otherwise, I chuck the slumped and oily cubes of buttternut squash, fennel, beetroot, carrot and potato into a frittata or roasted-vegetable tart.

Roast sausages with potatoes and grapes

12 good-quality sausages (pork, beef or venison)
500g potatoes, peeled and cut into 4cm pieces
12 shallots, peeled
500g red grapes
½ bulb garlic, cloves unpeeled
400g beetroot, quartered
3–5 tablespoons olive oil
salt and pepper

serves 6

Just as my mother used to cook steak and kidney pie once a week, I find myself rustling this up regularly, even though consistency and routine are not in my nature. It's Jamie Oliver in style; by that I mean you take one large heavy roasting tray, douse everything in olive oil and tons of fresh herbs and blast. I'd like to say 'Pukka', but I've heard he doesn't say that anymore!

Preheat the oven to 200°C/gas mark 6.

Put all the ingredients in a large roasting tin, slurp over the olive oil and seasoning and roast away for 45 minutes. You can't get easier than that.

You are left with a glorious claret-red sauce that could be reduced over a direct heat, with a knob of butter, to give you a gleaming glossy gravy.

Funghi forager's fry-up

400g mixed mushrooms
knob of butter
1 tablespoon olive oil
1 clove garlic, crushed
2–3 tablespoons flat-leaf
    parsley, torn
salt and pepper
juice and zest of 1 lemon
2 slices thick sourdough loaf

serves 2 as a snack on thick toast

Sorry about the title: it's quite late as I'm writing this and I can't work out if there's too much alliteration.

An Anglophile friend from Brittany, Kilda, finds chanterelles, ceps, the Hedgehog mushroom with it's white belly, the Scarlatina Bolete and the blue-hued Amethyst Deceiver, in the woods around Exeter in Devon. His funghi knowledge is far superior to mine. I only hope our current insatiable thirst for foraging won't be a fad and will, if you pardon the pun, mushroom into a deeper understanding of common edible funghi. Here in the UK I'd love to see mushroom ID posters in pharmacy windows in the autumn, as they have in France and Italy, especially after Nick Evans, the well-known author of *The Horse Whisperer*, who lives nearby, became critically ill last year after a mushroom mistaken identity. Take a knowledgeable friend or a mushroom guidebook and if, even after a process of funghi elimination, you are still not 100% sure of the identity of the mushroom, leave well alone.

Clean the mushrooms gently with a damp piece of kitchen paper. In a large frying pan over a moderate heat, melt the butter and olive oil. When the butter starts to foam fry the mushrooms for 4–5 minutes until gently coloured golden. Add the garlic during the last couple of minutes of cooking. Scatter with the parsley and season with lashings of salt, pepper, and lemon juice and zest.

Serve on lightly toasted sourdough bread so that the juices leach into it. If you prefer a lower carb hit, try 3 tablespoons of sourdough crumbs, sprinkled over the mushrooms on the plate.

Diggory's venison stew

1kg venison, chopped into
    2.5cm pieces

3 tablespoons olive oil or
    30g butter

2 tablespoons plain flour

2 medium onions, finely
    chopped

3 cloves garlic, crushed

1 red pepper, sliced

800g chopped tomatoes (2 cans)

200g mushrooms, sliced

1 glass red wine

10 sprigs of thyme

2 bay leaves

serves 5–6 generously

After a misty-morning canoe trip up the river Avon to Cockleridge, Digs bought a kilo of local venison and made this flavoursome autumnal stew, followed by Brownie Tart (see page 146). Some creamy mash, or some large, salted, slightly roughed-up potatoes would ride nicely alongside.

Preheat the oven to 150°C/gas mark 2.

Take a large, heavy, and probably quite expensive (don't drop it) casserole pan with a lid, and brown off the meat in the olive oil or butter over a moderate heat, until it leaves sticky patches on the bottom of the pan and has coloured the meat on the outside.

Put the rest of the ingredients into the pan, giving them all a stir through, then put on the lid and place the casserole in the oven for about 2½ hours. Have a peek occasionally – the meat should be tender, so that it comes apart easily with a fork, and the sauce should be a deep claret red and have thickened.

Brownie tart

200g unsalted butter, cut into
    pieces
85g dark chocolate
45g cocoa
250g caster sugar
3 eggs
2 teaspoons pure vanilla extract
70g plain flour
¼ teaspoon salt
100g mixed macadamia nuts,
    pistachios, Brazil nuts or
    almonds

for the ganache
50g dark chocolate, chopped
50ml double cream

enough for 5–6

I have long been attracted to the idea of a brownie tart, dotted with wells of liquid chocolate ganache. I have slightly anglicized the original American version and have omitted that perennial American favourite in bakery products – cream cheese – and have chosen to go for a package of mixed nuts instead. If you have any of the tart left over, it's great with a mid-morning latte and will have only got better by lunch time.

Preheat the oven to 160°C/gas mark 3.

Line a 23cm fluted tart tin that has a removable base with parchment paper.

Melt the butter and chopped chocolate together in a bowl over simmering water. When the chocolate has melted, transfer the mixture to a larger bowl.

Beat the cocoa, then the sugar, into the chocolate mixture until well blended. Add the eggs, one at a time, beating well after each addition, then the vanilla extract. Add the flour and salt and mix by hand until the flour is just incorporated. Stir in the nuts.

Place the tart tin on a large baking sheet (to catch any drips). Pour the brownie batter into the tart pan and spread it evenly with a spatula. Bake for about 30–35 minutes.

While the tart is baking make the ganache. Place the chopped chocolate in a small heatproof bowl. Heat the cream in a small saucepan over a moderate heat but remove it just before it boils. Immediately pour the cream over the chocolate and allow to stand for 5 minutes. Stir until smooth.

Remove the tart from the oven and place it on a wire rack to cool for about 5 minutes. Then, with the end of a wooden spoon that has been well greased, make holes in the surface of the brownie tart. As you insert the end of the wooden spoon into the tart, twist the spoon to prevent the tart from tearing. You should have about 25–30 small holes. Then, with a small spoon, fill the holes with the ganache. The ganache will sink as it cools, so top up as needed. Let the tart cool in the fridge.

Pudding, of the Victorian-nursery style, doesn't happen every night in our house. Sometimes it's fruit, a yogurt, a slither of chocolate or just an extra portion of main course. I thank my mum for my healthy approach to food in general and for my habit of not feeling guilty about having pudding. She would walk the dog or cycle us to school when we were younger. If I feel a bit stodgy, it's normally because I'm not being active enough, so I'll incorporate some running, cycling, walking or yoga into my week. There's a very direct cause-and-effect to that, which I like – a little like putting on a warm jumper if it's a bit chilly. In the winter, of course, some of these puddings can be considered warm jumpers themselves.

Rose-tinted rhubarb crumble cake

for the rhubarb
400g rhubarb stalks, cut to
  2.5cm pieces
3 tablespoons caster sugar

for the crumble
75g brown sugar
100g plain flour
75g butter

for the cake
125g butter, softened
220g caster sugar
3 eggs
250g plain flour, sifted
2 teaspoons baking powder
250ml sour cream

300ml double cream

serves 6–8

Yes, the rhubarb does sink to the bottom, but doesn't it leave a lovely rose-tinted stain as it does so?

Preheat the oven to 180°C/gas mark 4.

In a heavy-based pan, sauté the rhubarb pieces with 3 tablespoons of sugar and the merest splash of water. Set aside.

Mix together the brown sugar, plain flour and butter in a large bowl to form a crumble. Rub the fat gently into the flour until it resembles course sand with clots. Set aside.

Now make the cake batter. In a large mixing bowl or free-standing mixer, beat together the butter and caster sugar until pale, then add the eggs, sifted flour and baking powder, interspersed with the sour cream. Line a 23cm springform cake tin with baking parchment and spatula the mixture in. Place the rhubarb slices on top of the cake mixture and sprinkle with the crumble mix.

Bake in the oven for 45–50 minutes. Introduce the still-warm cake to a spoonful of double cream.

Other mid-week puds that don't require your undivided attention (which, frankly, at 6pm, is my reality) are: Cream of Ambrosia Rice Pudding (see page 21), which takes less than five minutes to prepare and put in the oven, Blackberry and Sour Cream Clafoutis (page 150, although I wouldn't have it after a toad in the hole), fresh fruit salad and fruit gratin with ice cream.

Fruit gratin

300g–350g fruit, such as
   blueberries, blackcurrants,
   blackberries, raspberries,
   stewed apples or cooked
   apricots
1 tablespoon caster sugar
3 tablespoons elderflower
   cordial
500ml custard
2 tablespoons demerera sugar

enough for 5–6

I struggle to think of a fruit, frozen or fresh, that would not work well in this context. Frozen fruit needs to be well defrosted and gently heated through. I generally use good-quality shop-bought vanilla custard for this. The general character of the dish was conceived, if not indeed fated, to be one of convenience. I reserve my custard-making skills for trifle, and Sundays.

Elderflower cordial provides an underlying floral aroma. It is great as an ingredient for sweet things, in the same way that you might use balsamic vinegar, or soya or Worcester sauce to enhance the savouriness, or *unami*, of a savoury dish.

Place the fruit in a 25cm-diameter pie dish. Sprinkle over the sugar and elderflower cordial. Top with the custard and demerera sugar. Under a really hot grill, cook for 5–10 minutes until the surface is blistered and golden brown. Serve straight from the grill in its cooking dish.

Blackberry and sour cream clafoutis

2 tablespoons plain flour

4 tablespoons caster sugar

seeds of 1 vanilla pod

3 eggs

125g sour cream

500g blackberries, fresh or
    frozen (or use raspberries or
    frozen forest fruits)

1–2 tablespoons icing sugar

feeds 4–5

As I write, the first autumn winds have started to blow and I love to make blackberry crumble and serve it with cream. Free food from the tangled hedgerows doesn't get much better. But as my Finn-inspired devotion to the 'Cult of the Berry' grows, so does my need to develop a less repetitive Sunday pud, or mid-week alternative to the usual bar of Green & Black's gobbled in front of the telly.

I've always loved clafoutis – the sweet echo of Yorkshire pudding – but minus the cherries. The addition of sour cream in the batter mix seductively echoes the runny cream you are about to pour over the whole ensemble.

A firm, cold slab of this also makes a fine mid-morning post-school-run breakfast for the needy and greedy.

Preheat the oven to 180°C/gas mark 4.

Whisk all the ingredients, except the fruit and icing sugar, in a large mixing bowl until you have smooth batter. Butter an ovenproof dish (the one I use for this is a 20cm-diameter terracotta dish) and scatter the fruit in so that it fits fairly snugly. Pour over the batter, then bake, uncovered, for 30–35 minutes. Sprinkle with icing sugar and serve with cream or ice cream.

Rahka

200ml whipping cream

250g Quark

250g berries (such as
    blueberries, strawberries,
    lingonberries or raspberries)

2–3 tablespoons caster sugar

1 teaspoon vanilla sugar

a neat portion for 4–5

I like to think of this as a kind of classless, Finnish Eton Mess. I have begun to appreciate the way Scandinavians and other Europeans use Quark. It is so much less artery-clogging than full-fat cream – although, saying that, I don't have any problem eating something like Eton Mess! This is another Finnish recipe that is perfectly aligned with their berry cult.

In a mixing bowl, whip the cream and stir through the Quark thoroughly. Gently stir in the berries and sprinkle in the sugars a tablespoon at a time. The degree of sweetness depends on the berries used and personal taste. This dish can be served chilled or at room temperature.

André Breton's early twentieth-century artistic definition of 'surreal' as being 'as beautiful as the chance encounter of a sewing machine and an umbrella on a dissecting table' seems slightly off-the-wall and something-stronger-than-caffeine induced.

Some of the most surreal food situations in this country are not found on the dissecting table, but on the British pub table, where you can find 50 different dishes from all corners of the culinary globe: Mexican alongside Thai, alongside a Ploughman's and a pint of cider!

My food in this chapter stems from many serendipitous situations: family day trips have influenced the creation of dishes such as Cliff Cake (see page 160), and even childhood stories, such as *Charlie and the Chocolate Factory,* have become the stimulus for new and risky dishes, such as Violet Beauregard's Cornish Pasty (see page 154). As 'post-modern' people, dare I say it, we are quite used to being eclectic in our everyday lives, seeing paint residue on a weathered piece of driftwood on the beach and wanting to translate the colour and texture to our bathroom wall, or finding a host of objects – striped feathers, a sea-worn shell, rusty metal – and being inspired to either paint a picture, design a dress or plant a garden encapsulating those ideas. For me, as a cook and artist, I would like to think that, sometimes, these interesting fragments can also lead on to the creation of a new cake, tart, stew or salad.

I'm often asked where I get the ideas for my recipes from. Paintings and books are certainly one source, and I don't mean just cookery books – some of the best pieces of food writing are in novels. Ian Fleming wrote some beautifully observed foodie passages in his Bond books, in between all the killing, and I was always entranced by Roald Dahl's sense of the absurd and fabulous in all food matters. As a child I fantasized about having the all-in-one chewing gum meal from Roald Dahl's *Charlie and the Chocolate Factory* that brings Violet Beauregard to an untimely, blueberry-hued end. I suppose the concept of the three-course dinner of soup, followed by roast beef and finished off, quite literally, with blueberry pie and cream, all coming from a thin strip of Wonka's magic chewing gum, fits well within my more surrealist notions of food.

Chance encounters
surreal food... including Violet Beauregard's Cornish pasty

Violet Beauregard's Cornish pasty

for the chicken and tarragon filling
500g diced chicken
1 tablespoon olive oil
50ml double cream
1 teaspoon loose tarragon,
    chopped
salt and pepper

for the lemon sponge filling
100g butter
100g caster sugar
2 eggs
100g self-raising flour
juice and grated zest of
    1 lemon
500g shortcrust pastry, made
    with 360g plain flour and
    180g cold butter (see page 8
    for method) or shop-bought
    is fine (you're doing enough
    here)
1 egg, beaten
2 tablespoons poppy seeds

enough for 6 pasties, 15cm long

I'm normally quite restrained, but the idea of making a modest two-course meal – in a sense, for the price of one – appealed to me. However, the more I thought about the idea, the more I realized it had already been done. This was of course the complete meal for Cornish miners: the two-course pasty, which has meat and vegetables at one end and fruit, such as apples, plums or cherries, at the other. Initially, I questioned whether the fruit ingredients could actually survive the lengthy baking process required for the meat so, to get around the problem of overcooking the sweet part of the pasty, I came up with a lemon sponge-pudding end, which takes pretty much the same time to cook as the chicken and leek end. I also wanted the 'whole meal' concept to follow through, so that the first 'course' was complemented by the desert! To avoid a lard-and-lemon combo I used butter for the pastry, which works well for a normal savoury pasty too. Adorned with poppy seeds, which complement the savoury chicken and sweet lemon ends, it is a summer jewel alongside its more rustic Cornish cousin.

These are best served still warmish – a little latent oven heat lingering on to the picnic. It's a good idea to put some kind of identifying mark on one end of the pasty – I do a sprinkling of poppy seeds on the chicken side – so that my twenty-first century 'miner' doesn't get his pud before his main.

Fry the chicken over a moderate heat in some olive oil for about 7–9 minutes, until cooked through. Add the cream, tarragon and seasoning, then remove from the heat and allow to cool.

In a mixing bowl, cream together the butter and sugar for the lemon sponge end of the pasty. Add the eggs and flour and mix well. Stir in the lemon juice and zest.

Preheat the oven to 180°C/gas mark 4. Roll out the pastry, then cut out six discs of pastry using a 15cm-diameter plate or bowl. Using the whisked egg, brush around the edge of each disc. Put a spoonful of the chicken filling on one quarter of each round, and

a spoonful of the lemon mixture on an adjacent quarter, so that the fillings together cover half of the pastry round. Bring the other half of the pastry round over the filling and crimp the edges with your fingers (or using a fork) to seal firmly. Brush with the beaten egg then demarcate with poppy seeds. Cut a couple of steam holes in the chicken side, to prevent splitting. Bake in the oven for 25 minutes, until the pastry is golden.

My A-list ingredients, aside from endlessly useful olive oil and Maldon sea salt, would be puy lentils, oodles of fresh herbs (outside in the summer and on the windowsill in winter), chilli, citrus and almond, maple syrup, and pumpkin seeds, to be sprinkled by the truck load onto crumbles, quiches and sweet tray bakes. Roquefort and Vacherin cheese would be there as well, in a kind of unapproachably beautiful capacity that won't mingle.

Green tart

250g shortcrust pastry, made using 180g plain flour and 90g cold butter (see page 8 for method), or use a shop-bought 20cm (8in) shortcrust pastry case
1 egg, beaten (for brushing)

for the filling
2 eggs
2 egg yolks
300ml double cream
salt and pepper
1 heaped tablespoon each of basil, thyme, chives, coriander and flat-leaf parsley
1 tablespoon pumpkin seeds

enough for 4–5

I had fun raiding lovely Tom's herb forest for this recipe. No euphemism intended.

Fistfuls of basil, thyme, chives, parsley and coriander are embraced and embedded in this tart, which seems like a resourceful way of using what many of us have outside our back doors growing freely. It also, to boot, makes the most of my favourite colour. Make sure the herbs are well cleaned; we don't want any mini beasts in here.

Have you noticed how Ofelia, the character in Guillermo Del Toro's beautiful Spanish Civil War film, *Pan's Labyrinth*, wears only shades of green while she is being repressed? I hasten to add that this is not a repressed tart in any way, but in fact an imaginatively liberated one.

Make the pastry and chill in the fridge for 30 minutes. Line a 20cm tart tin with it.

Preheat the oven to 190°C/gas mark 5.

Bake the pastry blind for 15 minutes, then remove the baking beans, prick the base, and return to the oven for 5 minutes. Brush with beaten egg and leave to cool. Reduce the oven temperature to 180°C/gas mark 4.

In a large bowl, whisk together the eggs, egg yolks and cream and season with salt and pepper. Stir in the chopped herbs, then pour the mixture into the waiting pastry case. Top with a sprinkling of pumpkin seeds and cook for about 25–30 minutes.

Jackson Pollock's meringues

400g caster sugar
200g egg whites (from about
   6 eggs)
1 vanilla pod
3 tablespoons fruit cordial, such
   as lavender, elderflower or
   pomegranate)

makes about 8 large meringues

Thank God all my expensive art-history education allows me to make connections between scrumptious sweet desserts and an American Abstract Expressionist painter. In truth, though, this isn't really inspired by the great Mr Pollock, but by the fabulous Ottolenghi in London. Ottolenghi's fruit-splattered or (more probably – but I'm not sure how) -sprayed meringues simply billow in the shop window.

Given some time, put on some trance-like music, clear the decks and splatter and spray away to your heart's content with the concentrated fruit juice – perfection!

Having made meringues by hand for years, I am now a complete convert to the charms of the free-standing mixer for creating billowing clouds of cumulus.

Preheat the oven to 200°C/gas mark 6.

Spread the sugar over a large baking sheet and bake in the oven for about 10 minutes until the sugar is warmed through and starting to dissolve from the edges in. Turn the oven down to 190°C/gas mark 5.

Get the egg whites whisking on full power in a free-standing mixer, then add the warm sugar. Add in the vanilla pod and beat for 10 minutes.

Place orange-sized mounds of the meringue mixture on a large baking sheet lined with baking parchment or a silicone sheet and cook for 1 hour 40 minutes, then switch off the heat and leave the meringues in the oven to cool down. This should give you a meringue that is dry on the outside but gooey on the inside.

Pour the fruit cordial into a small pan, bring to the boil and simmer for 5 minutes, until it has reduced by half. Using a spoon, splatter this thickened fruit syrup over the meringues. Serve with a warm berry compote, fresh fruit and cream.

Some of my favourite memories in life are food memories: eating take-away sushi at the top of the Empire State Building; bringing home *farina di castagne* (chestnut flour) from Tuscany, and soya sauce from Hong Kong (what was I thinking?); eating Keith Floyd's passion fruit *crème brûlée* by the sink window after a Michelin inspection had gone awry and the inspector left before dessert; and bringing home petrol-coloured live mussels from Rock in Cornwall.

Often, day trips are the ideal stimulus for abstracting a new dish inspired by a particular place. So at Lyme Regis, the dark, damp sedimentary rock strata says to me: some kind of chocolate cake with knobbly bits inside… maybe nuts, broken biscuits or dried fruit.

Cliff cake

150g biscuits (any mixture of digestives, shortbread and Italian biscotti will work)

200g chocolate (I use Green & Black's 'A darker shade of milk'; or use 100g milk and 100g dark chocolate)

150g butter

1 tablespoon golden syrup

grated zest of 1 orange

100g dried fruit (such as cranberries and apricots), chopped

150g nuts (such as pistachios, macadamia nuts, Brazil nuts and walnuts), chopped

chocolate vermicelli to decorate

enough for about 10 slices

It is no coincidence that I first made this cake when I returned from a family day trip to Lyme Regis. There should definitely be more responses to nature through the medium of food – as a kind of culinary Impressionism.

This cake has a split personality. It is part sophisticated North Italian spice cake – *Pampepato di Ciccolato*, as served by the Duke of Ferrara, Borso d'Este, at a Quattrocento banquet – and part trashy chocolate refrigerator cake. As you split open the cake, à la palaeontologist, it both veils and reveals its hidden treasures. It is only a short leap of faith to see the moist, enveloping chocolate as the dark, damp sedimentary rock of the Jurassic Coast (Dorset to you and me) and the shards of biscotti, moist fruit and pine nuts as Ammonites or Megalodon's teeth…T-rex bones perhaps? For the Duke of Ferrara's banquet, there was a real piece of gold inside each slice of cake.

The wonderful thing about this cake is that it dispenses with the need for an oven – just a little fridge time is all that is required. It could well be the perfect cake for the contemporary caveman or woman.

In the run up to Christmas, this is a good cake to have lurking in the fridge. It lasts ages and can be whisked out and sliced up as the unexpected drop in for a festive catch up. You can make a darker and slightly more sophisticated (not, perhaps, in the true sense of the word, but more in the *Ferrero Rocher* sense) version using dark chocolate and cocoa for dusting the top, or spice it up with dark chocolate, orange zest and chilli flakes.

Use clingfilm to line a 225g (½lb) loaf tin, leaving extra hanging over the sides; this helps to crane out the cake later.

Put the biscuits into a plastic bag, then bash the bag using a rolling pin, breaking the biscuits into shards. Try to stop bashing before it all turns to crumbs.

Melt the chocolate, butter and golden syrup together in a heatproof bowl set over a pan of simmering water. Stir occasionally. Remove the bowl from the heat and stir in the broken biscuits, orange zest, dried fruit and nuts.

Spoon the mixture into the prepared tin. Level the surface by tamping it down with the back of a spoon and sprinkle generously with the vermicelli; this is supposed to be the grass at the top of the cliff, after all. Cool in the fridge for 1–2 hours to set. Turn out the cake and peel off the clingfilm. Slice the cliff cake open.

An individual ingredient, such as the allotment-friendly broad bean, or an outstanding duo, such as citrus and almond, can be the point of departure for a familiar recipe to take on a whole new guise. In this way I realized that broad beans would probably make a damn good guacamole.

Broad bean guacamole

500g (unshelled weight) broad
   beans
1 clove garlic, crushed
½ teaspoon chilli
lemon juice

makes enough for 4 on the side

It's great to have a few broad bean recipes in your personal repertoire, particularly if you grow your own and need to use up the large, late-season mealy ones, whose sugar has turned to starch. Smashed up with garlic, chilli and lemon, it becomes a guacamole with low food miles, to be lavished on bruschetta or on good old British doorsteps. With their buttery mashable texture, similar to that of an avocado, and protein-rich flesh, supermarkets should really be making broad bean guacamole commercially in northern climes.

Cook the broad beans in plenty of boiling water for 4–5 minutes. De-case into a bowl using your fingers.

All the ingredients can now be put into a food processor and pulsed until you have the desired consistency; I like it with a few rough edges. Otherwise, place all the ingredients into a large mortar and tenderly grind to a paste with the pestle.

Macadamia pesto

75g macadamia nuts
1 clove garlic
40g coriander
1 tablespoon olive oil
1 tablespoon grated parmesan
juice of 1 lemon
salt and pepper

I'm a little weary of any old garlic-infused, sludgy herb mix becoming a 'pesto', but this addition to the canon, where gob-stopper-sized, buttery macadamia nuts take the place of petite pine kernels, is more than a nubbly sauce – it is a satisfying side dish for a fish, meat or vegetarian feast. With coriander standing in for basil, this pesto goes south of the Mediterranean. Purists would have a field day, although there is a fiery Sicilian version to be made using pecorino, mint, chilli and tomatoes.

Chop the nuts, garlic and coriander finely, then mix together all the ingredients in a mortar and grind to a rough paste using the pestle (or blitz in a food processor; but don't go too fine).

Rocket and buttermilk soup

225g chorizo, sliced
200g feta cheese, crumbled
2–3 tablespoons olive oil
1 large leek, white part only,
    finely chopped
500ml chicken stock
2 small potatoes, chopped into
    small cubes
200g rocket (1 large bunch)
285ml buttermilk
salt and pepper

serves 6

My friends Rachel and Tom of Old Cumming Organic Farm grow seductive salad leaves and have a field full of rocket. This soup is homage to their beautiful produce and lovely family. It's great with lightly fried chorizo and crumbled feta to give it a salty edge. (I have also made in parallel a successful vegan twin using vegetable stock and soya milk.) This vibrant soup will make you ready for post-lunch pursuits and put off the siesta (or fat-man's nap, as we say in the West Country) for another day.

Fry the sliced chorizo in about 2 teaspoons of olive oil over a medium heat, until it is slightly coloured at the edges and has a bit of crunch. Set this aside with the crumbled feta for later.

Heat the remaining olive oil in a large, heavy pan over a moderate heat. Add the leek and cook until soft and translucent. Add the chicken stock and potatoes and cook for about 20 minutes, until the potatoes are soft. Put the rocket leaves into the pan and boil for a couple of minutes, then plunge the pan into a sink of cold water. This stops the buttermilk you are about to add curdling.

Blitz the soup with a hand-held blender until smoothish. Stir in the buttermilk and season. Serve in bowls with lightly fried chorizo and crumbled feta.

I love to embrace food from other people's travels, as well as my own. Something cherished in its original incarnation, such as porchetta from the Marche in Italy, can be transformed into an everyday mid-week meal, and the mere mention of an intriguing fish soup from Zanzibar, puts me into Google-mania mode as I research the type of ingredients to try using in order to create my own.

Zanzibar fish soup

3 tablespoons olive oil

4 shallots, finely chopped

2 sticks celery, finely chopped

3 cloves garlic, crushed

5cm length of fresh root ginger, peeled and grated

1 red chilli

200g canned chopped tomatoes

600ml water

375ml dry white wine

2 bay leaves

2 strips of orange peel

pinch of saffron

500g fresh whole fish, steaks or fillets (skate, bass, bream, coley, mullet, gurnard and pollock are good choices)

1kg mussels

100ml double cream

1 handful of coriander, chopped

8 spring onions, sliced

serves 5–6

My beautiful sister-in-law lusted after this soup before she climbed Mount Kilimanjaro recently (she lusted after a gorgeous chap from San Francisco, during and after her climb, but that's another story, with a very happy ending, I might add). She ate it, loved it, climbed to the icy summit, found the recipe in a book (*A Kitchen Safari*), and then passed it on to me. The fantastic thing about this dish is that you don't need any fancy 'grown or flown in from Zanzibar' ingredients. Fish that will hold its shape during cooking – mullet, gurnard, pollock or similar – and home-grown mussels are all great here. The addition of a starchy carbohydrate such as rice or millet, something that can slowly sink into the soup, makes it a satisfying lunch or supper dish.

Heat the olive oil in a large saucepan, then add the shallots, celery, garlic, ginger and chilli. Cook over a moderate heat until soft, but do not let the mixture brown. Add the tomatoes, water, white wine, bay leaves, orange peel and saffron and bring to the boil. Simmer for 10 minutes.

Add the fish to the pot and cook, still simmering, for another 15–20 minutes, then throw in the mussels and cook for 5 minutes, until the shells open; discard any that remain closed. Remove the soup from the heat, then stir in the cream, coriander and spring onions. Ladle away.

Potato lasagne

for the ragu sauce

2 tablespoons olive oil

2 medium onions, very finely chopped

2 celery stalks, very finely chopped

1 red pepper, finely chopped

1kg minced beef

1 glass of red wine

2 x 400g canned plum tomatoes

1 glass warm milk

for the béchamel

600ml milk

55g butter

75g flour

100ml double cream

brief grating of nutmeg

250g fresh lasagne

200g mozzarella, sliced

100g parmesan, finely grated

handful of fresh basil, torn

4 large waxy potatoes, such as Charlotte or Ratte, cooked and sliced

enough for 6–8

This is the logical conclusion of nearly 20 years of lasagne making. The topping of mozzarella and a parmesan crust evolved in Sydney, where we discovered that parmesan had the effect of not only providing a salty top note, but also a ceiling under which the mozzarella melts and pretends it's a soufflé. I'm not sure of the chemistry going on in the oven, but I do enjoy the result.

The other strange and, some might say, completely unnecessary addition to the well-trodden lasagne canon is the using of left-over waxy potatoes from supper the night before. The potato adds an extra starchy note, absorbing a little of the two sauces and simultaneously thickening them; work that one out. It was created in a farmhouse in Tuscany, so it feels authentic.

I completely embrace the mellowing addition of milk in the ragu sauce, a wonderful gift to all cooks from Anna Del Conte and Marcella Hazan.

First make the ragu sauce by heating the olive oil in a large, heavy pan. Add the chopped onions, celery and red pepper, and continue to cook over a moderate heat, stirring frequently, until they are soft; this should take about 7–9 minutes. Add the minced beef and cook until it no longer has any rose-coloured or raw patches. Add the wine and boil energetically for 2–3 minutes, until it has reduced slightly. Add the canned tomatoes and simmer for 10 minutes. Warm the milk in a small pan, pour over the meat sauce and stir. Cook for a further 2 hours on a low heat, stirring and tasting as and when the mood takes you.

While the ragu is still cooking, make the béchamel sauce. First warm the milk in a pan to just-before-boiling point. Meanwhile, heat the butter in a heavy-based pan over a low heat. Stir in the flour – I use a balloon whisk for this. Take the pan off the heat and whisk in the hot milk, a few glugs at a time, making sure that the flour has blended with the milk before each new addition. Grate in the nutmeg and return the pan to the heat. Stirring constantly, cook for a further 7–10 minutes until the sauce has thickened and the flour has cooked. Remove from the heat and stir in the cream.

Preheat the oven to 200°C/gas mark 6.

In an ovenproof baking dish that's about 20cm x 30cm, spread a thin layer of the ragu on the bottom, cover with a layer of lasagne (2 whole sheets with a small gap in between works), then a layer of béchamel and another layer of ragu. Follow this with a layer of potatoes then repeat the ragu-lasagne-béchamel layering. Finally lay over the slices of mozzarella and sprinkle generously with grated parmesan and some torn basil leaves.

Bake in the oven for 20–25 minutes. Remove from the oven and let the lasagne stand for at least 5 minutes before serving – this will develop the flavours and make it easier to lift a piece out. We normally eat this with a green salad the first day, then re-heated on its own for lunch the next.

Porchetta meatballs

1 medium onion, finely chopped
500g sausage meat
2–3 tablespoons fennel seeds
100g polenta, plus extra for
  dusting
1 tablespoon olive oil

serves 4 with pasta

I had a porchetta epiphany in the Marche recently, about half an hour inland from Rimini. It is how I imagine Tuscany to have been 50 years ago, before mobile telephone masts became the most prominent feature of mediaeval hilltop villages.

I love meatballs in all their guises, from the chilli-flecked North African to the dill-infused Swedish and the Mediterranean herb-rolled. At some times of the year it is difficult to get hold of good minced pork, or sausage meat, so around Christmas, when the shops are brimming with it, I stockpile tubes in the freezer.

Combine all of the ingredients except the olive oil in a large mixing bowl and mix together robustly with a fork. Make into golf-ball-sized meatballs and finally roll in polenta to prevent sticking. Allow to rest in the fridge for 30 minutes to firm up.

Fry the meatballs in the olive oil over a low to moderate heat in a large frying pan for 10–15 minutes until they are brown on the outside. Break into one and check the inside is cooked through.

We enjoy these with silky strips of pappardelle pasta and a scant tomato sauce made from a finely chopped onion, some garlic, and a can of tomatoes reduced with whatever fresh herbs are hanging around.

Salmon dauphinoise

2 leeks, white part only, finely
  chopped
25g butter
800g salmon fillets
1kg potatoes
560ml double cream
300ml milk
2 cloves garlic, crushed
salt and pepper
handful of fresh dill, chopped

serves 4–5

This Swedish/French hybrid feels so right. It seemed to me a logical trajectory from the classic Swedish dish Jansson's Temptation (in Swedish, *Jansson's Frestelse*), which uses sprats or, more commonly, anchovies to make this version using salmon. Jansson was a religious fanatic who vowed to renounce earthly pleasures. For more earthly pleasures… keep reading.

Fry the leek in the butter until meltingly soft. Set aside. Preheat the oven to 180°C/gas mark 4.

Bake the salmon on a baking sheet for about 10 minutes (depending on its thickness). Ideally, it will still have semi-translucent flesh in some parts, but be easy to flake. Remove from the oven and set aside. Turn the oven down to 140°C/gas mark 1.

Peel the potatoes and slice them into 5mm-thick slices. Put in a bowl of cold water and set aside. Pour the cream and milk into a pan and add the garlic and seasoning. Warm over a low heat and remove just before the liquid comes to the boil, then stir in the chopped dill. Set aside. Drain the potatoes and pat dry.

In a shallow gratin dish or roasting tray that measures roughly 20cm x 30cm, layer the potatoes and salmon (starting with the potatoes), dredging with warm cream and a sprinkling of leek as you build up the layers. Cover with foil and bake for an hour until the potatoes are soft. Remove the foil in the last 10 minutes, to give a burnished top.

Double fennel and beetroot tart

2 fennel bulbs

500g beetroot with leaves intact

1 tablespoon fennel seeds

3 tablespoons olive oil

2 large red onions, sliced from tip to tip

1 clove garlic, crushed

375g shortcrust pastry (shop-bought is fine)

100g goat's cheese, sliced into rounds

black salt (see page 186)

10 sprigs of thyme, leaves picked off

serves 5–6

This might sound like a double-fronted aniseed attack, with both fennel seeds and fennel bulbs, but the roasting mellows and sweetens the bulbs like nobody's business. The 'black' salt is a bit poncy, but looks fantastically stark against the pale white rounds of goat's cheese, in the way that poppy seeds and hemp could also. It's pretty much impossible to cut petite slivers of this tart as the topping is fairly weighty, so go ahead and slice into generous rustic portions.

Preheat the oven to 200°C/gas mark 6. Slice each bulb of fennel through the root into four wedge-shaped segments and cut the beetroot into 1.5cm cubes. Tear the beetroot leaves and set aside. Place the fennel and beetroot chunks together in a roasting tray and scatter over the fennel seeds and 2 tablespoons of the olive oil. Roast for 35–40 minutes, then remove from the oven to cool. Turn down the oven to 180°C/gas mark 4.

174

While the fennel and beetroot are roasting, cook the sliced onion and garlic in a tablespoon of olive oil over a low to moderate heat for about 20 minutes, until soft. Set aside to cool.

Roll out the shortcrust pastry to cover an oven shelf-sized baking sheet. Arrange the onion, roasted fennel and beetroot, and goat's cheese rounds on the pastry. Scatter with black salt, fresh thyme and torn beetroot leaves and bake for 25–30 minutes, until the pastry is cooked.

A sausage and apple tart for New Year

250g shortcrust pastry, made using 180g plain flour and 90g butter (see page 8 for method)

50g butter

1 large onion, sliced

500g sausage meat

100g breadcrumbs

2 apples, peeled, cored and chopped

1 heaped tablespoon chopped flat-leaf parsley

salt and pepper

serves 6–8

If nothing else, my personal mantra has to be 'buy extra sausage meat at Christmas' so that you can freeze it, then make this at the end of January when the detox has finished. The trimmings of the festive feast are so often viewed as the best part of the festive dinner – here they *are* the dinner.

At the beginning of *Chitty Chitty Bang Bang*, when the children go off to the beach with a picnic, they try to tempt Truly Scrumptious to come with them by enticing her with their mixed up picnic of 'sausage tarts and marmalade rolls'. I like to think that my sausage tart could happily coexist in that dream-like, celluloid reality.

Preheat the oven to 180°C/gas mark 4. Line a 30cm tart tin with the pastry and bake blind for about 10 minutes.

Melt the butter in a frying pan over a low heat and fry the onion, stirring occasionally, until softened but not coloured. Pour the cooked onions into the pastry case with the sausage meat, breadcrumbs, apple pieces, parsley and a good seasoning of salt and pepper.

Cook in the oven for 30–35 minutes.

Chocolate swizzlers

100g dark or milk chocolate
(with around 40% cocoa
solids)
lolly sticks

*makes 4–6 swizzler sticks,
depending on the size of the
ice-cube tray used*

This seems an inaccurate name for something that really twizzles in a cup of hot milk, although I sense 'twizzler' as a culinary adjective probably doesn't give a favourable first impression. Ironically, the turkey twizzler that has been so reviled is clearly, obviously, one big swizzle! I feel like Willy Wonka making these, but could do with some Oompa Loompas to help break up the chocolate.

Melt the chocolate in a bowl set over a pan of simmering water; it doesn't have to melt until it is completely smooth, as a few grits in it will hold the lolly stick in place. Spoon the melted chocolate into the recesses of an ice-cube tray and insert a lolly stick into each one. Leave to set in the fridge.

When completely set you should be able to remove the chocolate cube, with the lolly stick intact, and use it to stir into a cup of hot milk to create a delicious cup of hot chocolate.

Provence on the rocks

An undeniably kitsch, summer drink that can be enjoyed simultaneously as adult fizz (prosecco) and child fizz (lemonade) at Pimms-o'clock.

Fill a third of any wine glass or tumbler with lavender cordial and top up with either lively Prosecco or fizzy lemonade, and ice.

When I went into hospital to have my first baby, I packed a family-sized plastic tub full of dark chocolate-loaded brownies. I thought that I would probably need and deserve them, and looked forward to coming home to a freezer stuffed with lasagnes and crumbles for the first hectic week with a newborn in the house. If I was doing the baby thing now, I'd probably stash some Caramel Salties in my bag amongst the newborn all-in-ones and respectable pyjamas.

Caramel salties

250g golden caster sugar
100g butter
200g caramel or Dulce de Leche
2 eggs
200g self-raising flour
100g white chocolate, chopped
   into large chunks
2–3 teaspoons salt

makes about 8 slices; although I always double the recipe (as shown in picture opposite)

Diggory gave me an exquisite box of salted caramels from Melt, in London's Notting Hill, for my birthday. Little balls dusted with cocoa that held inside a dark liquid caramel laced with gritty Maldon sea salt. I would have loved to have gorged on them, but since there were only 16 of these little beauties, I rationed myself to two a day and prolonged the pleasure.

We're all familiar with chocolate brownies and pale blondies, but caramel salties? Salt and sweet is such a good combination and little saline pyramids of Maldon salt in these provide an uplifting inflexion to the richness beneath. Children might prefer that you leave half the slab without salt, if you are up for sharing, that is.

Halen Môn, the fabulous salt producer from Anglesey, makes wonderful Welsh sea salt flakes with Tahitian vanilla, and you can also buy Cornwall's own sea salt harvested from the aquamarine water's off The Lizard (see page 186 for details of suppliers).

Preheat the oven to 180°C/gas mark 4. Line the bottom and the sides of a 25cm x 25cm brownie tin or small roasting tin with baking parchment.

In a large mixing bowl or a free-standing mixer (it's on my Christmas list, again), beat the sugar and butter until pale, then add 150g of the caramel, the eggs, then the flour. Stir in the white chocolate, then put the mixture into the brownie tin. Dab blobs of the remaining caramel onto the surface, like you would mozzarella on a pizza. Sprinkle with a fine dusting of sea salt and bake for 20–25 minutes. As with any member of the brownie 'family', it's ready when the edges are cooked and the middle is still a tad sticky. Remember – it will keep cooking even after it has been removed for the oven.

It was Nigella Lawson who guided me to the online joys of joyofbaking.com. If I ever want to check out a generic recipe for a muffin or tart that can be tinkered with to suit my culinary whim, I do a pit-stop here. The site, part food blog, part comprehensive bakery project, reflects the positive life spirit of its creator Stephanie Jaworski.

Chocolate caramel muffins

dry mix
260g plain flour
250g caster sugar
2 teaspoons baking powder
½ teaspoon salt
60g cocoa
200g caramel chocolate (the kind that has caramel encased in milk chocolate), chopped into large pieces

wet mix
250g ricotta
2 large eggs
320ml milk
60g butter, melted

makes about 18 medium-sized muffins

My eldest son always asks 'Mum, did you really invent these?' Insofar as coming up with the idea for trying out gob-stopper-sized caramel chocolate chunks in a moist chocolate muffin recipe, then the answer is 'Yes'. It's not really up there with the first wheel though, I admit.

These mini Krakataus have little epicentres of molten caramel. I rose at about 4am on a boat on the way from Sumatra to Java to catch a glimpse of 'big K' – I saw lots of flying fish (very Dr Seuss) but no Krakatau. It was on that trip that I had one of the most surreal food experiences for breakfast, a legacy of Dutch colonialism: white cardboard bread, butter and, for sprinkling on top, a bowl of hundreds and thousands. Techno meets Mother's pride head on. I digress.

There are lots of online retailers who sell coloured baking-parchment muffin cases (see page 186 for details of suppliers). These ones, made by hand, may not be stylish but are wonderful by virtue of being beautifully translucent, and they also support the muffin as it rises during baking.

Preheat the oven to 180°C/gas mark 4. In no particular order, put all the dry-mix ingredients into a large bowl. In a measuring jug, measure the milk first, then stir in the other wet ingredients.

Pour the wet mix from the jug onto the dry mix in the bowl and stir together gently with a wooden spoon. The wet and the dry mixtures need to be amalgamated, but overall do not need to be supremely smooth. A few lumps tend to be good for the texture of the finished muffin.

Spoon the thick mixture into the muffin cases (if you don't make your own, use standard-sized shop-bought cases) set in muffin tins and bake for 20–25 minutes, until springy.

Rose petal and buttermilk cake
(otherwise known as The Big Fat Fairy)

for the cake
125g butter, softened
250g golden caster sugar
2 eggs
250ml buttermilk
1 teaspoon vanilla extract
250g plain flour, sifted
pinch of salt
2 teaspoons baking powder

for the icing
250g golden icing sugar
2 tablespoons boiling water
seeds of 1 vanilla pod

50g crystallised rose petals

cuts into 10–12 slices

Having been asked to make iced fairy cakes one day and, feeling too lazy to fiddle about with individual cases, I made a big one – hence the name (apologies to any big fat fairies reading). The basis for this is the lovely smiley Bill Granger's beautiful Buttermilk Cake. This is a good, solid, but also incredibly soft cake that will hold its shape for icing. I love buttermilk in cakes and bread. Try adding a dollop to a basic white bread mixture for a baby-soft interior.

With a single candle this is the perfect oversized cupcake for an adult's birthday. I like to decorate mine with vanilla-dirty golden icing and a sprinkling of crystallised rose petals. This is best served (more of an ogress – and less a goddess – moment) in its own giant pleated fairy-cake case with a big mug of tea for a truly through-the-looking-glass moment.

Preheat the oven to 180°C/gas mark 4. Cream together the butter and sugar in a large mixing bowl or free-standing mixer. Add the eggs one at a time, mixing well after each addition. Now beat in the buttermilk and vanilla extract. Add the sifted flour, salt and baking powder gradually.

Spoon evenly into a 20cm springform cake tin lined with baking parchment. Bake for 40–45 minutes until the surface is golden and a skewer (or piece of dry spaghetti) inserted into the centre of the cake comes out clean.

In a large bowl, mix the sifted icing sugar with 2 tablespoons of boiling water and the vanilla seeds until lump free. Spread onto the cake and decorate with crystallised rose petals.

Chocolate bark

100g chocolate (white, milk or
    dark)
suggestions for toppings:
    macadamia nuts, vanilla
    seeds, rose petals, apricots,
    Brazil nuts, orange zest...

Like an edible Rosetta Stone, these chocolate tablets can be
designed by the eye – or led by the store cupboard. Some good
combinations are white chocolate with lavender and lemon zest,
vanilla with Hunza apricots and macadamia nuts, and cardamom
with edible rose petals.

This recipe is just crying out for creative input: try and design
some new pictograms with the nuts and sprinkles and watch
your guests as they decipher your Codex Cocoa.

Line the base of a 225g (½lb) loaf tin with baking parchment: this
will be the mould for the chocolate tablet.

Melt the chocolate in a bowl set over a pan of just-simmering
water. When completely melted, pour into the mould. The
chocolate needs to be 3–5mm thick. Sprinkle with the chosen
toppings and leave to set at room temperature.

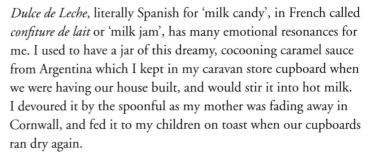

Dulce de Leche ice cream

200ml milk
400g Dulce de Leche (or use a
   397g tin of Carnation Caramel
   – don't worry about the
   absent 3g)
400ml double cream
seeds of 1 vanilla pod

Dulce de Leche, literally Spanish for 'milk candy', in French called *confiture de lait* or 'milk jam', has many emotional resonances for me. I used to have a jar of this dreamy, cocooning caramel sauce from Argentina which I kept in my caravan store cupboard when we were having our house built, and would stir it into hot milk. I devoured it by the spoonful as my mother was fading away in Cornwall, and fed it to my children on toast when our cupboards ran dry again.

I was excited about having invented this ice cream in my sleep. But later in the day, as I tried to order the main ingredient online, I was crushed to discover that Häagen-Dazs had beaten me to it! However, this is still worth making as it doesn't require the more labour-intensive custard base of most creamy ice creams. Having some competition from big HD only strengthened my resolve. It's well up to the mark.

Bring the milk and Dulce de Leche just to the boil in a heavy saucepan set over a moderate heat, then remove from the heat and whisk in the cream until it has dissolved. Whisk in the vanilla seeds and transfer the liquid to a metal bowl. Quick-chill by putting the bowl in a sink of ice-cold water (stirring the liquid occasionally) until cold.

Now transfer the mixture to an ice-cream maker or an airtight container and put in the freezer. While it is still semi-frozen, remove it from the freezer once an hour for the first three hours and give it a good stir, then leave it in the freezer until it freezes completely. Take the ice cream out of the freezer 15 minutes before serving.

Unusual ingredients

Below is a list of ingredients, some of which may be unfamiliar, so I have provided notes on where you might search them out.

Andouille: Try a French deli, or substitute with a medium-coarse French pork salami.

Agave nectar (sometimes called agave syrup): Try this as a substitute for golden syrup for a sugar-reducing option. Use it for drizzling over porridge, too. It releases energy more slowly than sugar, is nutritious, has a low GI, and is much sweeter than sugar, so less is needed. I can get it in my local health-food shops, and it's emerging into mainstream supermarkets – Waitrose/Ocado definitely stock it, and I recently found some in Morrisons supermarket.

Black salt: Try Indian grocers' shops for this, or Morrisons supermarket.

Cloudberry jam: This can be bought from online retailers such as swedishjuice.com and organicdelivery.co.uk, and also at Ikea food shops, where it's called Sylt Hjortron.

Crystallised rose petals: These are sold in clear plastic jars in the cake decorating/sprinkles section of most major supermarkets (I've bought them from Morrisons, Tesco, Sainsbury's, Waitrose – the lot; they are surprisingly easy to find). Normally, you'll find them next to the crystallised violets!

Eucalyptus honey: Good supermarkets will stock this, and if you find it at farmers markets, you may well get to try it first.

Edamane beans: These are soya beans and are readily available from supermarkets alongside the frozen peas.

Herb salt: Supermarkets do sell herb salt mixes, but I make it from fresh herbs for Roast Chicken with Herb Salt and Sage Puddings (see page 18).

Lavender cordial: Made by Rocks, this can be bought in many supermarkets and independent shops.

Orange flower water: Most mainstream supermarkets stock this – you'll find it next to rose water and near vanilla extract.

Pomegranate molasses: This is simply pomegranate juice boiled down to a thick dark syrup, sometimes with added sugar. It is used in salad dressings, sauces, gravies and even cakes. Again, Morrisons are selling it, which suggests other supermarkets would have it. Middle Eastern delis, health food shops and farm shops are also good places to try.

Rapadura sugar: One of my latest discoveries at my local farm shop is organic rapadura sugar. This is unrefined sugar with the consistency of fine sand, that is made from dehydrated raw cane juice from unburnt sugarcane. Unlike refined sugars, it is full of nutrients and has a seductive caramel aroma that complements sweet baking. I use it as a substitute for regular caster sugar in some recipes, for a smokier and less sweet fix. Try health-food shops and farm shops to source rapadura sugar, or search for it online.

Savoiardi biscuits: You can get Savoiardi biscuits at Tesco and all supermarkets (sometimes they are simply called 'sponge fingers') and even a local Spar!

Za'tar: Visit the brilliant www.seasonsedpioneers. co.uk for this – they call it Zahtar. Try supermarkets – Waitrose stock it, made by the brand Bart.

Stockists and suppliers

I tend to think of Devon as the Tuscany of the North, and most of my suppliers are local. Most undertake national – and some, international – delivery. For details of farm shops visit www.farmersmarkets.net.

Baking: For coloured and patterned muffin cases and sprinkles that come in a variety of shapes and colours, try www.cakescookiesandcraftsshop.co.uk.

Herbs and spices: For a cornucopia of chilli products, try www.southdevonchillifarm.co.uk. For wonderful spice mixtures and a good place to get freshly ground cardamom for Korvapuusti (see page 54), visit www.seasonedpioneers.co.uk.

Meat: South Devon Meat from Aune Valley (www.aunevalleymeat.co.uk) supply good-quality meat, as do the aptly named www.wellhungmeat.co.uk. Perhaps the brilliant Riverford meat boxes from www.riverfordmeatbox.co.uk would suit your needs.

Salt: Mostly, I use Maldon Salt, which can be found easily in most supermarkets. I can also recommend Halen Môn, a wonderful sea salt from Anglesey (www.seasalt.co.uk). I'm also a big fan of Cornish Sea Salt (www.cornishseasalt.co.uk).

Vegetables: When he's not chatting on Radio 4 and ranting in his brilliant newsletters about the omnipotence of supermarkets, Guy Watson is putting together his brilliant family veg and fruit boxes from the family's pioneering Riverford box scheme (www.riverford.co.uk). Fabulous salad leaves and juice can be had from Old Cumming Organic Farm, available through south west farm and health food shops.

Bibliography

Listed below are all my 'virtual' friends, the books from chefs and cooks that I spend time re-reading and cooking with. They include titles from Bill Granger, whose casual fresh food evokes an idealized life in Sydney; Tessa Kiros with her vast and personal repositories of culinary memory; Nigella Lawson (particularly *Feast* to lift my spirits); and Nigel Slater, who sits fairly permanently, in all his guises, beside my bed!

Cantor, David and Kay, and Swann, Daphne: *The Cranks Recipe Book*, 1982
Day-Lewis, Tamasin: *The Art of the Tart*, 2000
del Conte, Anna: *Gastronomy of Italy*, 2001
Granger, Bill: *Sydney Food*, 2000
——: *Bill's Food*, 2002
Hughes, Kathryn: *The Short Life and Long Times of Mrs Beeton*, 2005
Jansson, Tove: *The Summer Book*, 1972
Kiros, Tessa: *Falling Cloudberries: A World of Family Recipes*, 2004
——: *Venezia: Food and Dreams*, 2008
Lawson, Nigella: *Feast: Food That Celebrates Life*, 2004
——: *Forever Summer*, 2002
Ndlovu, Dumi, and Short, Yvonne: *A Kitchen Safari: Stories & Recipes from the African Wilderness*, 2004
Ottolenghi, Yotam, and Tamimi, Sami: *Ottolenghi: The Cookbook*, 2008
Slater, Nigel: *Appetite*, 2000
——: *Tender*, 2009
Watson, Guy, and Baxter, Jane: *Riverford Farm Cook Book: Tales from the Fields, Recipes from the Kitchen*, 2008
Wright, John: *River Cottage Handbook 1: Mushrooms*, 2007

The photography

I have learned on the job to be a food photographer. My father was a professional photographer, although I probably didn't listen to him enough, and I am surrounded in my circle of family and friends by outstanding photographers in different genres. Along the way I have invented my own tools of the moment: a large shiny saucepan lid angled to reflect a little bit more of the late evening light onto the Italian Wedding Soup; a handy olive oil dispenser for drizzling spots and creating puddles at the bottom of bowls and to encourage the colours of the sky onto glossy salad leaves; greaseproof paper as a great waxy light diffuser, and children's hands – well they look so much better than mine.

I scrambled up onto a boundary wall to get the last of the September light, when I was taking the pictures for the Sweet Red Onion Tart with Goat's Cheese in a nearby village. The elderly woman next door quickly pulled down her kitchen blind – maybe she thought I was some kind of burglar in reverse, about to force my tart on to her.

I really understand why photographers say it's all about the light. The day of the flapjack shoot, just below the headland on the beach, it was disappointingly misty, but the resulting images have an ethereal quality to them, where the mist has gently diffused the light, making the flapjack sing.

Acknowledgements

I feel lucky and truly grateful to have landed on planet Hardie Grant and find myself in the experienced and nurturing hands of publishing ace, Jane Aspden, and also to have been introduced to the *other* Miranda, Miranda Harvey, whose light touch on her Mac produces jaw-dropping spreads and excited faces all round. I am also indebted to Salima Hirani, my wonderful recipe editor and late-night email correspondent.

Mary Bekhait at Limelight Management – thanks for starting this thing, and for being supportive and instinctive from the outset.

I owe deep heartfelt thanks to friends for their kitchens, conversations and spontaneous meals, particularly talented photographer Tom Benn (www.bennphotos.co.uk), Catrin Evans, Lizzie and Jem, Heather Morris and Penny Lindeque. To Loulou – thanks for being the perfect friend and temporary neighbour, and allowing me to remove dinner plates from your table, just as you are about to eat, for another photo. Also to Rachel and Tom Brooks from Old Cumming Organic Farm for their wonderful produce, lovely girls and open house; and to Sarah at Gazebo, Totnes, for her wonderful Scandinavian kitchen accessories and for letting me go into her lovely shop and say 'I'll have that and that and that...': www.whatalovelyshop.co.uk. Thanks also to Debby Mason (www.debbymason.com) for allowing me to reproduce her wonderful mackerel print on the cover of this book.

Thanks to my family, who will be relieved to have me back eating and cooking family meals without a pair of cameras around my neck, hunting the right light with a plate of food in hand. Digs, thank you, thank you, thank you. My children: Beren – 'Will we be eating everything out of your book?' Me (reflecting on last couple of years): 'We just did.' Raz: 'Mum, can we try caramel sorbet?' Me (towards deadline): 'I think that will have to wait for the next book!' Magi: 'Mum, can we have this every night? It's better than beans.'

To the family at large: I am grateful to Simon, for the wonderful house he has built us and, with Emily, for their big-hearted family meals, Emma for wonderful flowers and rose petal confetti (www.emmavowles. co.uk), Felix and Brian, and also to Lucy for constantly inspiring us with her desire to see the world. Thanks also to Diane for her unlimited support and for being the perfect 'Nana', Dad for being the inspiration for this book, and Team-Finland: Dexter, Leena, Oskari, Harold and Ukko.

Lastly, I thank my trusty camera, a modest black Lumix with a lovely Leica lens – I thought I had lost you at Lulworth Cove. And thank you to my long-serving laptop: though you contain many of the children's cake crumbs, you continue to serve!

Miranda Gardiner
Devon 2009